Help Me! Guide to the Kindle Fire HDX

By Charles Hughes

Table of Contents

Getting Started

Table of Contents

1. Button Layout

The Kindle Fire HDX has three buttons, a headphone jack, and a micro-USB port. The touchscreen is used to control all functions on the Kindle Fire HDX, with the exception of turning on the device and controlling the volume. The Kindle Fire HDX has the following buttons:

Figure 1: Front View

Touchscreen - Used to control all functions on the Kindle Fire HDX.

Figure 2: Rear View

Power Button - Turns the Kindle Fire HDX on and off, locks, and unlocks the device.
Volume Control - Increases and decreases the media volume.

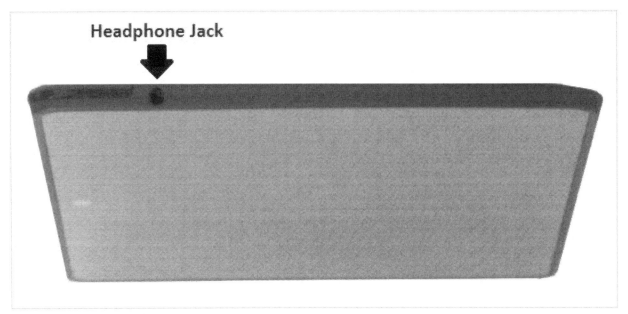

Figure 3: Right Side View

Headphone Jack - Allows headphones to be connected to the Kindle Fire HDX to listen to audio.

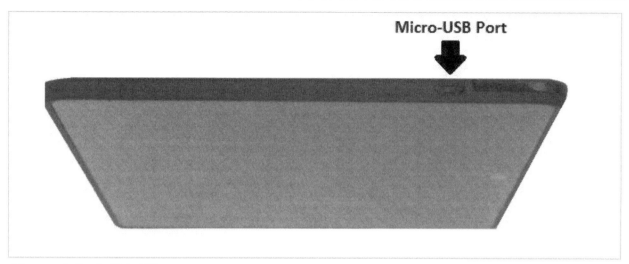

Figure 4: Left Side View

Micro-USB Port - Connects the Kindle Fire HDX to a computer to transfer data.

2. Charging the Kindle Fire HDX

For optimal battery life, charge the Kindle Fire HDX fully before using it for the first time. You can charge the device in one of two ways: use the Micro-USB charger, such as the one that comes with the Kindle Fire HDX (recommended method), or use the USB to Micro-USB cable included with your device to plug the device into any USB port on a computer. Note that the device will charge much more slowly when connected to a computer.

Note: There is no way to tell whether the device is fully charged by looking at the Home screen or Lock screen. Refer to "Displaying the Current Battery Percentage" *on page 253 to learn how to determine whether the battery is fully charged.*

3. Turning the Kindle Fire HDX On and Off

To turn the Kindle Fire HDX on, press the **Power** button on the back of the device and immediately release it. The Kindle Fire HDX turns on. When the device is fully turned on, the Lock screen appears.

To turn the Kindle Fire HDX off, press and hold the **Power** button for two seconds. The Shut Down confirmation appears, as shown in **Figure 5**. Touch **Power off**. The Kindle Fire HDX turns off. Alternatively, touch **Cancel** if you wish to keep the device turned on.

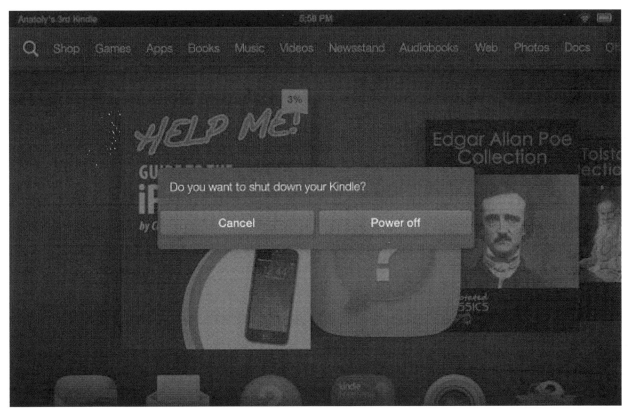

Figure 5: Shut Down Confirmation

4. Setting Up the Fire HDX for the First Time

The first time the Kindle Fire HDX is turned on, it must be set up. To perform first-time setup:

Note: If your Kindle Fire HDX came registered to the account you used to purchase it, steps 6 and 7 below are not required.

1. Press the **Power** button at the bottom of the screen and immediately release it. The Kindle Fire HDX turns on and the Language screen appears after a few moments, as shown in **Figure 6**.
2. Touch a language in the list, and then touch **Continue**. The Wi-Fi Networks screen appears, as shown in **Figure 7**.
3. Touch a network in the list. The Network Password prompt appears, as shown in **Figure 8**.

4. Enter the password for the Wi-Fi network that you selected, and touch **Connect**. The device connects to the selected network, provided that the password is correct. The Account Confirmation screen appears, as shown in **Figure 9**. By default, you will be registered under the Amazon account that you used to purchase the device. If you wish to select another account, touch **Not MYNAME**, where MYNAME represents the name under which you registered for the Amazon account, and then enter your Amazon credentials.
5. The Amazon Prime screen appears. Touch **Get Started** if you wish to sign up for the service, or touch **No thanks, continue without Prime** to use the device without the Prime service. The Social Network screen appears, as shown in **Figure 10**.
6. Touch a social network in the list to connect to it. Enter your credentials on the following screen to connect to one of these networks. If you wish to proceed without connecting to a social network, just touch **Next**. The Kindle Fire HDX setup is complete, and your device is ready for use.

Note: The device may need to download additional software before you can use it.

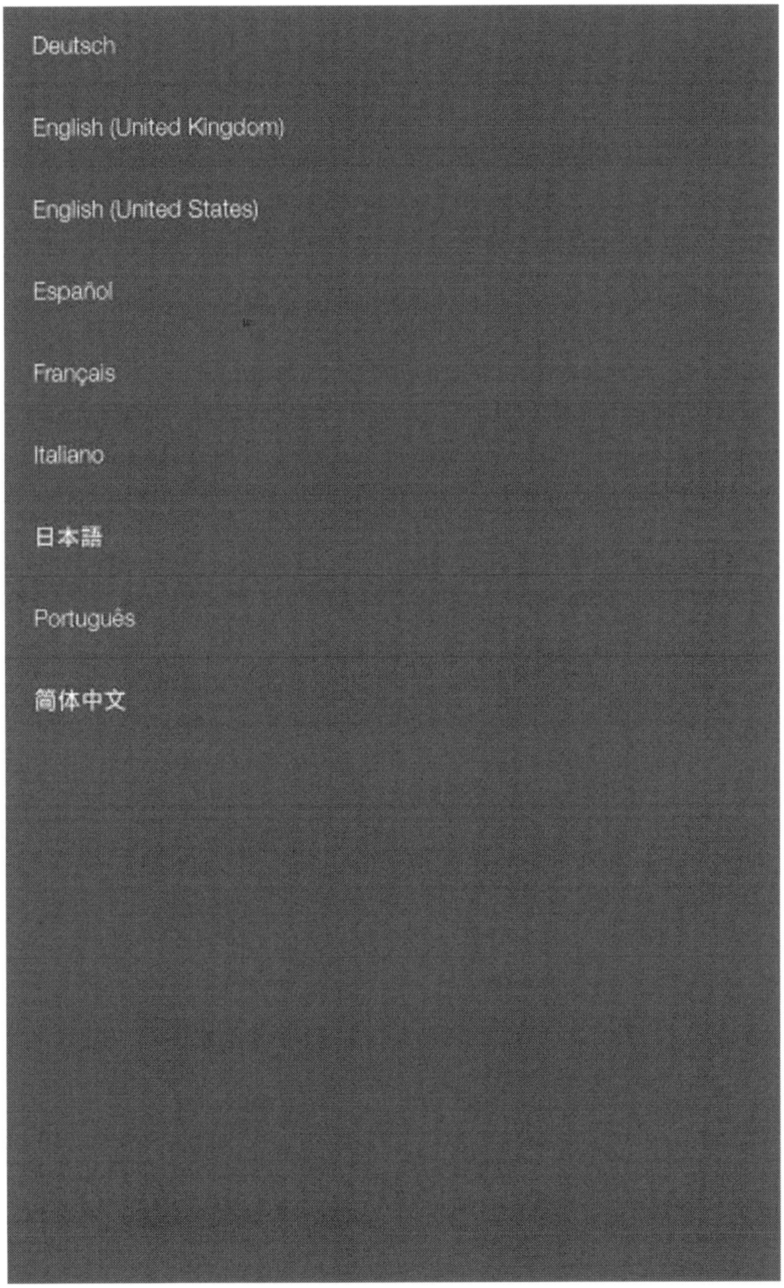

Figure 6: Language Screen

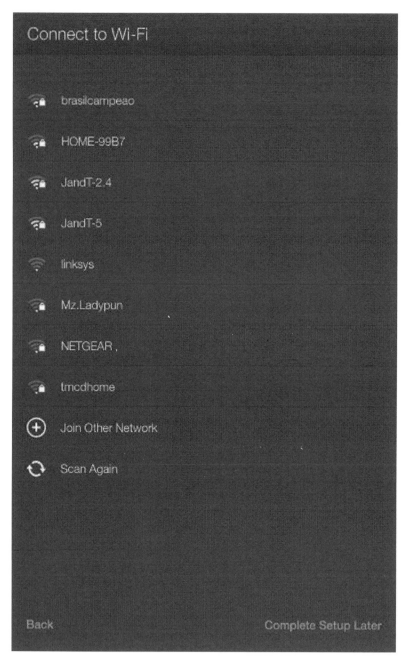

Figure 7: Wi-Fi Networks Screen

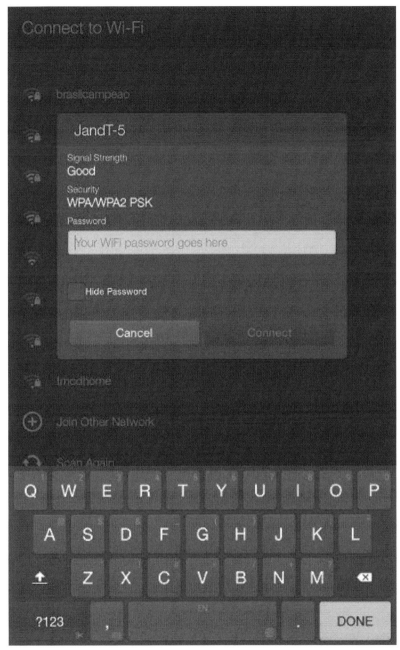

Figure 8: Network Password Prompt

Figure 9: Account Confirmation Screen

Figure 10: Social Network Screen

5. Deregistering and Re-registering the Kindle Fire HDX

If your Kindle Fire HDX came registered to an Amazon account other than your own, you may wish to re-register it. To deregister and re-register the Kindle Fire HDX:

1. Touch the time at the top of the screen and slide your finger down. The Notification Center appears, as shown in **Figure 11**.
2. Touch the ⚙ icon in the upper right-hand corner of the screen, as outlined in **Figure 11**. The Settings screen appears, as shown in **Figure 12**.
3. Touch **My Account**. The My Account screen appears, as shown in **Figure 13**.
4. Touch the [Deregister] button. A confirmation dialog appears.
5. Touch the [Deregister] button again. The Kindle Fire HDX is deregistered and the new My Account screen appears.
6. Touch the [Register] button. The Registration screen appears, as shown in **Figure 14**.
7. Enter the email address and password associated with your Amazon account and touch the [Register] button. The Kindle Fire HDX is registered to your Amazon account.

Figure 11: Notification Center

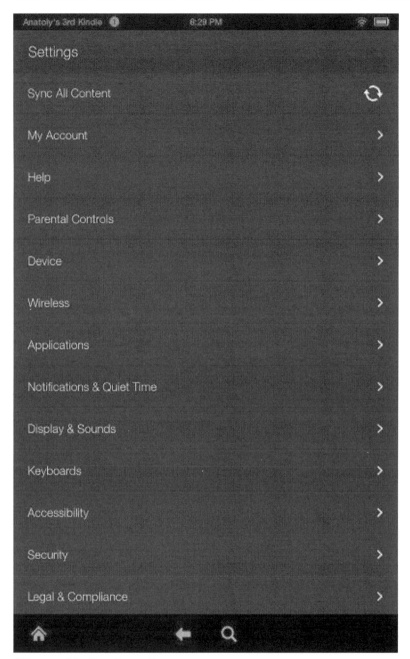

Figure 12: Settings Screen

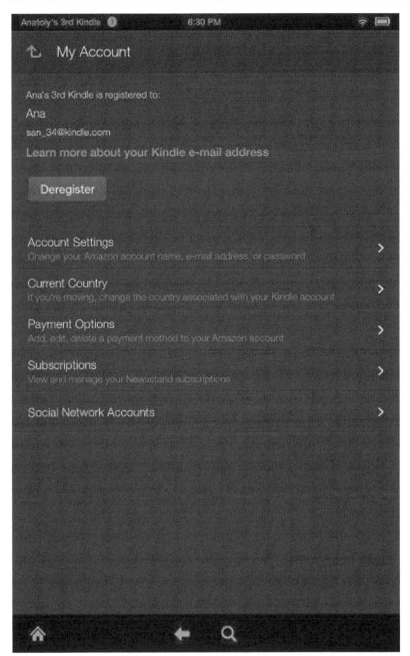

Figure 13: My Account Screen

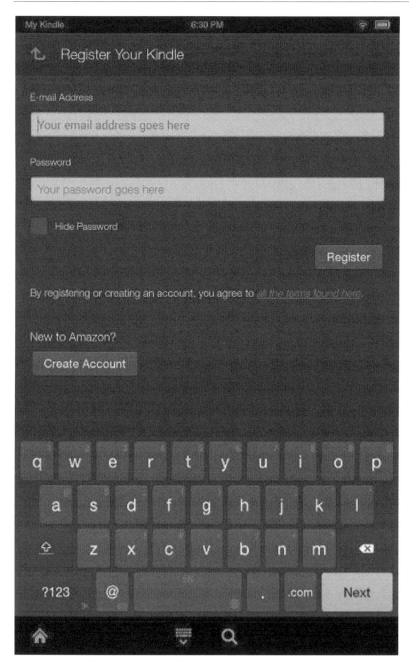

Figure 14: Registration Screen

6. Navigating the Screens

There are many ways to navigate the Kindle Fire HDX. These are just three of the methods:

- Touch the ⌂ button to return to the Library at any time. Any application or eBook will be in the same state when it is re-opened.
- Touch the ⬅ button to return to the previous screen or menu, or to hide the keyboard.
- Touch the left edge of the screen and slide your finger to the right to open the navigation menu.

7. Connecting the Kindle Fire HDX to a PC or Mac

eBooks and other files that you have obtained elsewhere can be imported to the Kindle Fire HDX. To import media:

1. Connect the Kindle Fire HDX to your computer using the provided USB cable. Your computer will make a sound or a notification will appear in the lower right-hand corner of the monitor to notify you that the device is connected.
2. Open **My Computer** on a PC and double-click the 'KINDLE Portable Media' removable drive. On a Mac, you will need to download the Android File Transfer utility, which can be found at **http://www.android.com/filetransfer/**. The Kindle Fire HDX folder opens.
3. Double-click **Internal Storage**. The Kindle Folders open on a PC, as shown in **Figure 15**, or on a Mac, as shown in **Figure 16**.
4. Double-click a folder. The folder opens.
5. Drag and drop a file into the open folder. The file is copied and will appear in the corresponding library.

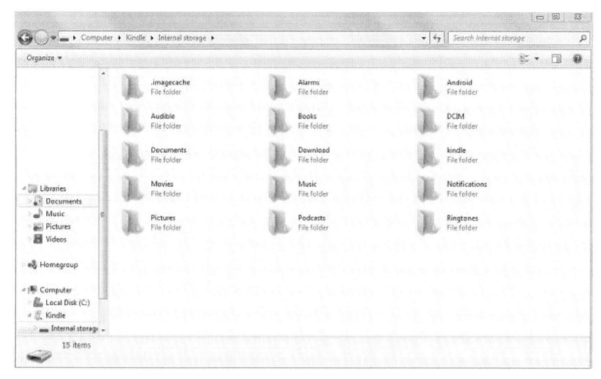

Figure 15: Kindle Folders on a PC

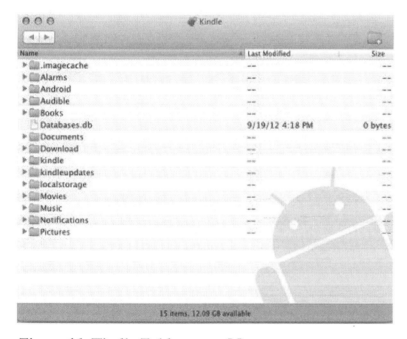

Figure 16: Kindle Folders on a Mac

Managing eBooks and Periodicals

Table of Contents

1. Buying an eBook on the Kindle Fire HDX

You can buy an eBook from the Amazon Kindle Store using your Kindle Fire HDX. To buy an eBook:

Warning: Before touching BUY, make sure that you want the eBook. The Kindle Store uses one-click purchasing. Once you leave the Confirmation screen, you cannot cancel the order.

1. Touch **Books** at the top of the Home screen. The Books Library appears, as shown in **Figure 1**.
2. Touch **Store** in the upper right-hand corner of the screen. The Kindle Store opens, as shown in **Figure 2**.
3. Touch the 🔍 icon at the top of the screen, as outlined in **Figure 2**. The virtual keyboard appears at the bottom of the screen.
4. Enter the name of an author or eBook and touch the [Q] key. A list of matching eBook results appears, as shown in **Figure 3**.
5. Touch the title of an eBook. The eBook description appears, as shown in **Figure 4**.
6. Touch **Buy for $##.##** where the ##.## represents the price of the eBook. The eBook is purchased and downloaded to your Kindle Fire HDX Library.
7. Touch the [Read Now] button to read the eBook immediately. The eBook opens.

Note: Touch **Cancel Order** *below the* 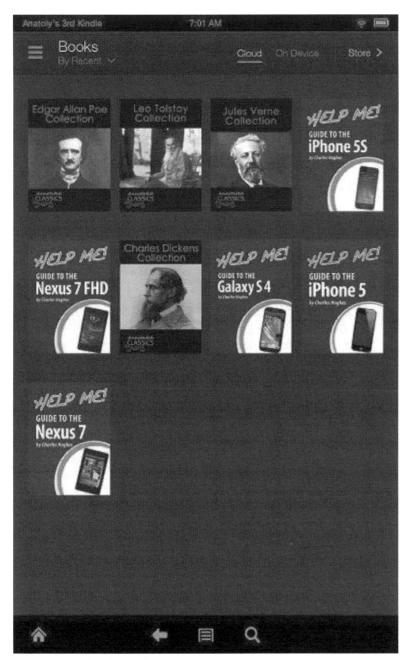 *button on the Confirmation screen if you did not mean to purchase the eBook. You cannot cancel the order once you have left the confirmation screen.*

Figure 1: Books Library

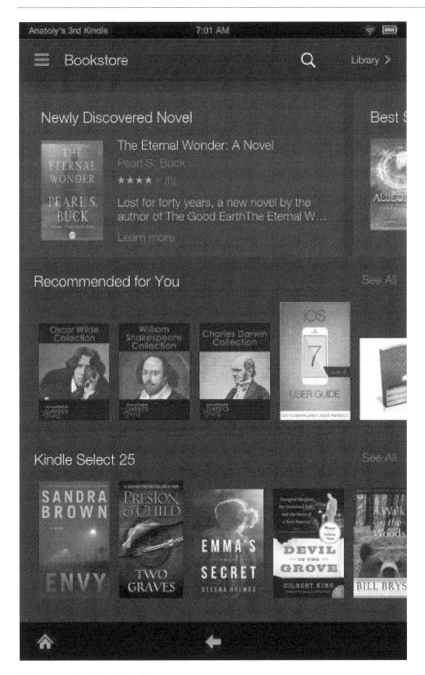

Figure 2: Kindle Store

Figure 3: List of Available eBook Results

Figure 4: eBook Description

2. Buying or Subscribing to a Periodical

You can buy or subscribe to a newspaper or magazine from the Kindle Store using your Kindle Fire HDX. To buy or subscribe to a periodical:

Warning: Before touching the **Buy Issue** *button or the* **Subscribe now** *button, make sure you want the periodical issue. The Kindle Store on the Kindle uses one-click purchasing. Unlike with eBook orders, you will not be given an opportunity to cancel a periodical order from the Confirmation screen.*

1. Touch **Newsstand** at the top of the Home screen. The Newsstand Library appears, as shown in **Figure 5**.
2. Touch **Store** in the upper right-hand corner of the screen. The Newsstand Store opens, as shown in **Figure 6**.
3. Touch the [search icon] icon at the top of the screen, as outlined in **Figure 6**. The virtual keyboard appears at the bottom of the screen.
4. Type the name of a periodical and touch the **Return** key. A list of matching periodical results appears, as shown in **Figure 7**.
5. Touch the title of a periodical. The Periodical description appears, as shown in **Figure 8**.
6. Touch the **Buy Issue** button to purchase an issue or touch the **Subscribe now** button to subscribe. A confirmation is shown and the periodical issue appears in the Library. You have 14 days to cancel your subscription before you are charged for the first time. Refer to *"Cancelling Your Newspaper or Magazine Free Trial"* on page 35 to learn how to cancel your subscription.

Figure 5: Newsstand Library

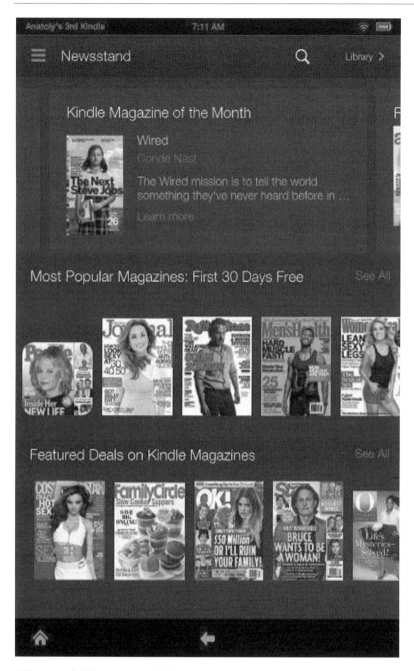

Figure 6: Newsstand Store

Figure 7: List of Matching Periodical Results

Figure 8: Periodical Description

3. Cancelling Your Newspaper or Magazine Free Trial

To cancel a subscription to a newspaper or magazine, use the Amazon website on your computer or Kindle Fire HDX. To cancel a subscription:

1. Go to **www.amazon.com/myk** using your computer's internet browser or the Amazon Silk browser on the Kindle Fire HDX. If you are signed in, the Kindle Information screen appears, as shown in **Figure 9**.
2. Click **Subscription Settings**, outlined on the left side of the screen in **Figure 9**. The Subscription Settings screen appears, as shown in **Figure 10**. Your active subscriptions are shown on this screen.
3. Click the `Actions... ▼` button next to the subscription you wish to cancel. The Subscription options appear.
4. Click **Cancel Subscription**. A confirmation window appears.
5. Click the `Cancel Subscription` button. The subscription is cancelled.

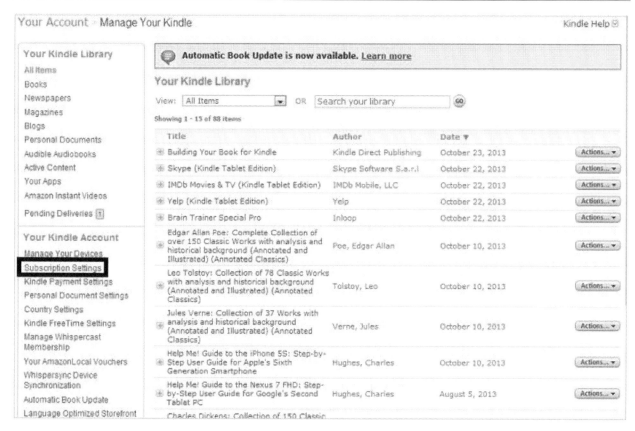

Figure 9: Kindle Information Screen

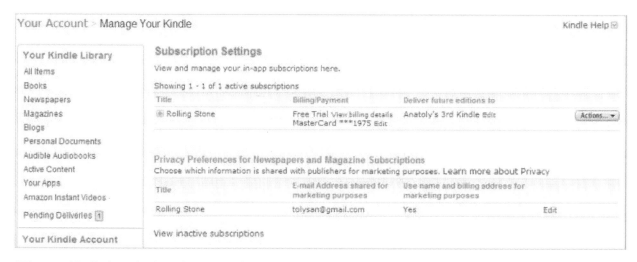

Figure 10: Subscription Settings Screen

4. Browsing Recommendations

Amazon makes recommendations based on the eBooks you have viewed or purchased. To view these recommendations:

Note: Only the Kindle Store offers customized recommendations. The Newsstand Store does not have this feature.

1. Touch **Books** at the top of the Home screen. The Books Library appears.
2. Touch **Store** in the upper right-hand corner of the screen. The Kindle Store opens.
3. Touch **See more** next to 'Recommended for You'. A list of recommendations appears, as shown in **Figure 11**.

Note: Refer to "Buying an eBook on the Kindle Fire HDX" *on page 25 to learn how to purchase an eBook.*

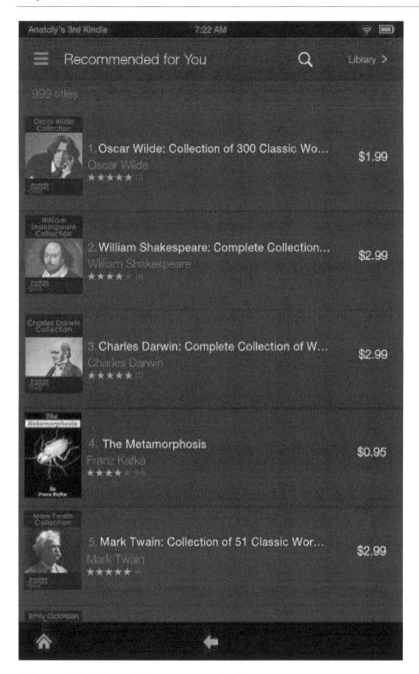

Figure 11: List of Recommendations

5. Buying an eBook on Amazon.com Using Your Computer

In addition to using the Kindle Fire HDX, eBooks can be purchased online at Amazon.com using your PC or Mac and then transferred to your tablet. Refer to *"Connecting the Kindle Fire HDX to a PC or Mac"* on page 23 to learn more. To search for and purchase an eBook on Amazon.com:

Warning: Before clicking 'Buy now with 1-Click', make sure you want the eBook. The Kindle Store on Amazon.com uses one-click purchasing. Once you leave the Confirmation screen, you cannot cancel the order.

1. Go to **www.amazon.com** using your computer's Web browser.
2. Point your mouse cursor at **Shop by Department**. A list of departments appears.
3. Point your mouse cursor at **Books & Audible**. The Books Categories appear, as outlined in **Figure 12**.
4. Click **Kindle Books**. The Kindle Store opens and the eBook categories appear on the left side of the screen, as shown in **Figure 13**.
5. Click a genre in the Books menu on the left side of the screen. Keep clicking genres on the left side on the following screens. A list of eBooks is shown each time. Search for a specific eBook or author by clicking on the Search drop-down menu.
6. Click the eBook that you wish to purchase. The eBook Description screen appears.
7. Select the name of your Kindle from the 'Deliver to' drop-down menu. Your Kindle is selected.
8. Click **Buy now with 1-Click**. A Confirmation screen appears and the item is delivered to your Kindle.

Note: A purchased eBook is only delivered to the device selected in step 7. To download the eBook to another registered device, open the Archived items and restore it. Refer to "Archiving an eBook or Periodical" *on page 41 to learn how to restore an eBook on the Kindle Fire HDX.*

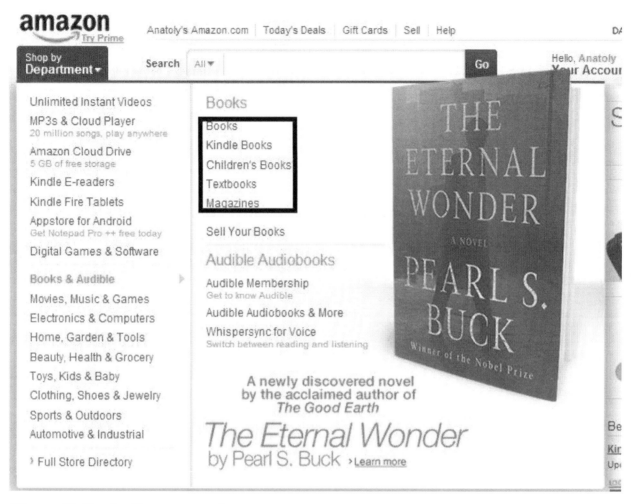

Figure 12: Books Category on Amazon.com

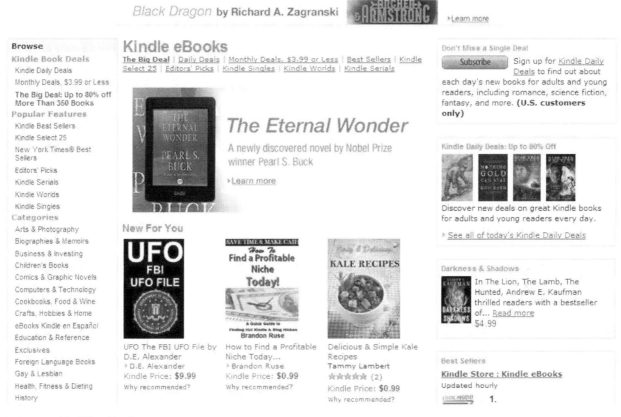

Figure 13: Kindle Store

6. Archiving an eBook or Periodical

An eBook or periodical can be removed from your Kindle and placed in the Amazon Cloud where it does not take up space on your device. An archived eBook is retrievable using the wireless connection. To archive an eBook or periodical, touch and hold its cover on the Home screen or in the corresponding library. The Item menu appears, as shown in **Figure 14** (Home screen) and **Figure 15** (Books library). Touch **Remove from Device**. The eBook or periodical is archived in the Amazon Cloud.

Note: To restore an archived eBook, touch **Cloud** *in the Books library and then touch the eBook cover.*

Figure 14: Item Menu on the Home Screen

Figure 15: Item Menu in the Books Library

7. Keeping a Periodical Issue when a New Issue is Downloaded

When you have a subscription to a periodical, you can have the Kindle Fire HDX either delete the previous monthly issue every time a new one arrives or keep the issue. To retain the previous periodical issue, touch and hold the cover on the Home screen or in the Newsstand library. The Item menu appears. Touch **Keep**. The issue will be kept when a new one is downloaded. To automatically delete the current issue, touch and hold the cover again. The Item menu appears. Touch **Do not Keep**. The issue will be deleted when a new one is downloaded.

Note: By default, the Kindle Fire HDX will automatically delete the previous issue when a new one is downloaded.

8. Searching for an eBook in the Library

If you have a large number of eBooks on your Kindle Fire HDX, you can find a specific eBook more easily by searching your library. To search for an eBook:

1. Touch **Books** at the top of the Home screen. The Books Library appears.
2. Touch the icon at the bottom of the screen. The virtual keyboard appears.
3. Enter the title or author of an eBook. A list of matching library results appears, as shown in **Figure 16**. Touch the title of an eBook to read it.

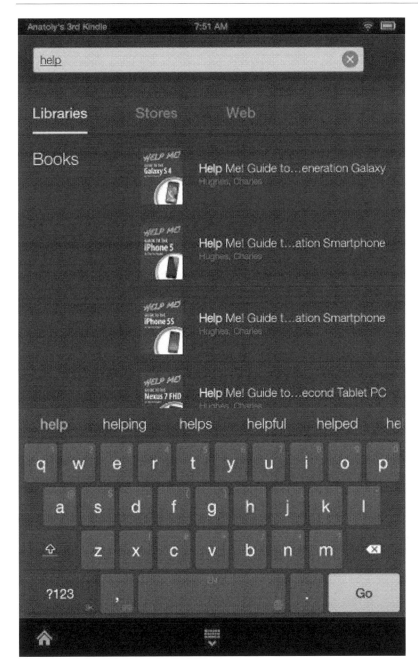

Figure 16: List of Matching Library Results

9. Sorting eBooks in the Library

You may organize the eBooks in your library chronologically by the download date, by author, or by the title. To sort your eBooks:

1. Touch **Books** at the top of the Home screen. The Books Library appears.
2. Touch **Books** in the upper left-hand corner of the screen. The Sort menu appears, as shown in **Figure 17**.
3. Touch **By Author**, **By Recent**, or **By Title**. The eBooks are sorted accordingly.

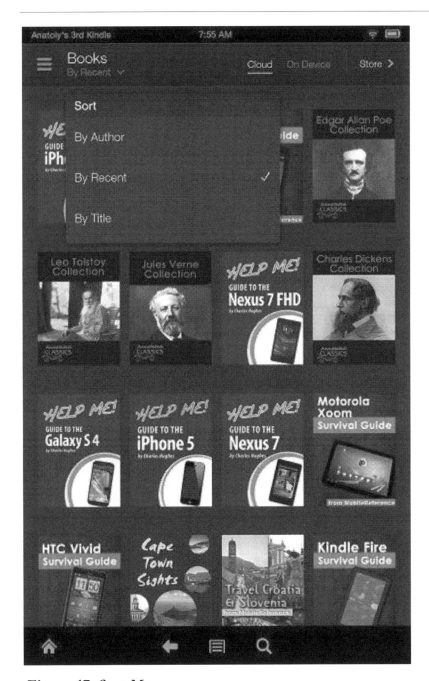

Figure 17: Sort Menu

Reading eBooks and Periodicals

Table of Contents

1. Navigating an eBook or Periodical

The Kindle Fire HDX makes it easy to navigate an eBook or periodical. Use the following tips while reading:

- **Navigating the Pages** - Touch the screen and move your finger to the left to turn to the next page or to the right to turn to the previous one.
- **Navigating to a Specific Location** - Touch the screen anywhere (as long as it is not a link). The eBook menu appears at the top of the screen. Touch the ⬤ on the ▬▬▬▬▬●▬▬▬▬▬ bar at the bottom of the screen, and drag it to the left or right to select a specific location in the eBook or periodical.
- **Sync to Furthest Page Read** - Touch the left edge of the screen and slide your finger to the right. The eBook menu appears, as shown in **Figure 1**. Touch **Sync to Furthest Page Read**. The device opens the furthest read page, using all devices registered to the same Amazon account as references.
- **View in Image in Full-Screen Mode** - Touch an image twice in quick succession.

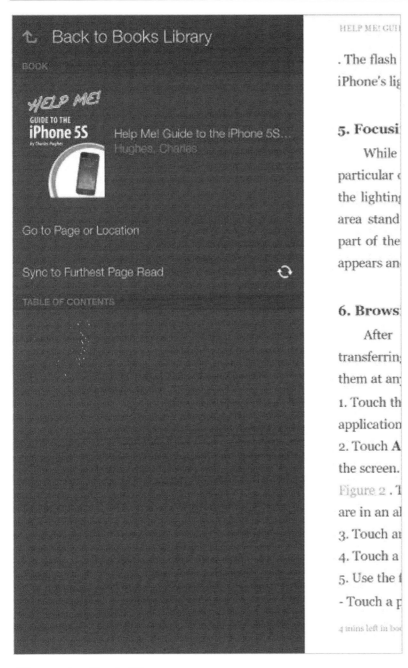

Figure 1: eBook Menu

2. Looking Up a Word in the Dictionary

While reading an eBook or periodical, use the built-in dictionary to look up word definitions. To look up a word, touch and hold it. A quick definition appears, as shown in **Figure 2**. Touch **Full Definition**. The full dictionary definition appears, as shown in **Figure 3**. Touch the ◁ button at the bottom of the screen to resume reading where you left off.

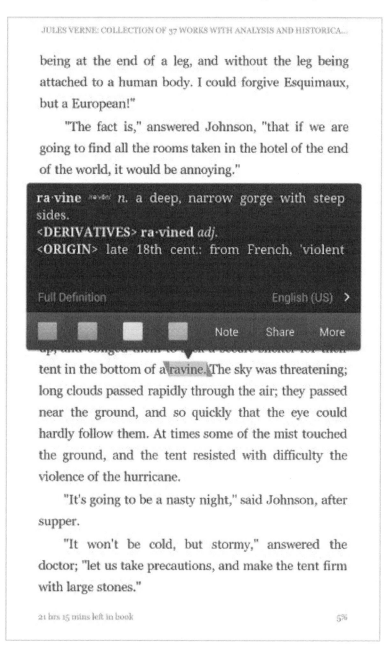

Figure 2: Quick Definition

Figure 3: Full Dictionary Definition

3. Highlighting a Word or Phrase

While reading an eBook or periodical, words and phrases can be highlighted. To highlight a word or phrase:

1. Touch and hold a single word until the magnifying glass appears, as shown in **Figure 4**. You may now select the text that you wish to highlight.
2. Drag your finger without letting go of the screen to select a phrase or release the screen to highlight a single word. The phrase is selected and the Text menu appears, as shown in **Figure 5**.
3. Touch one of the colors (pink, blue, yellow, or orange) in the menu. The word or phrase is highlighted, as shown in **Figure 6**.

Note: Refer to "Viewing Your Notes, Highlights, and Bookmarks" *on page 58 to learn how to view your list of highlights.*

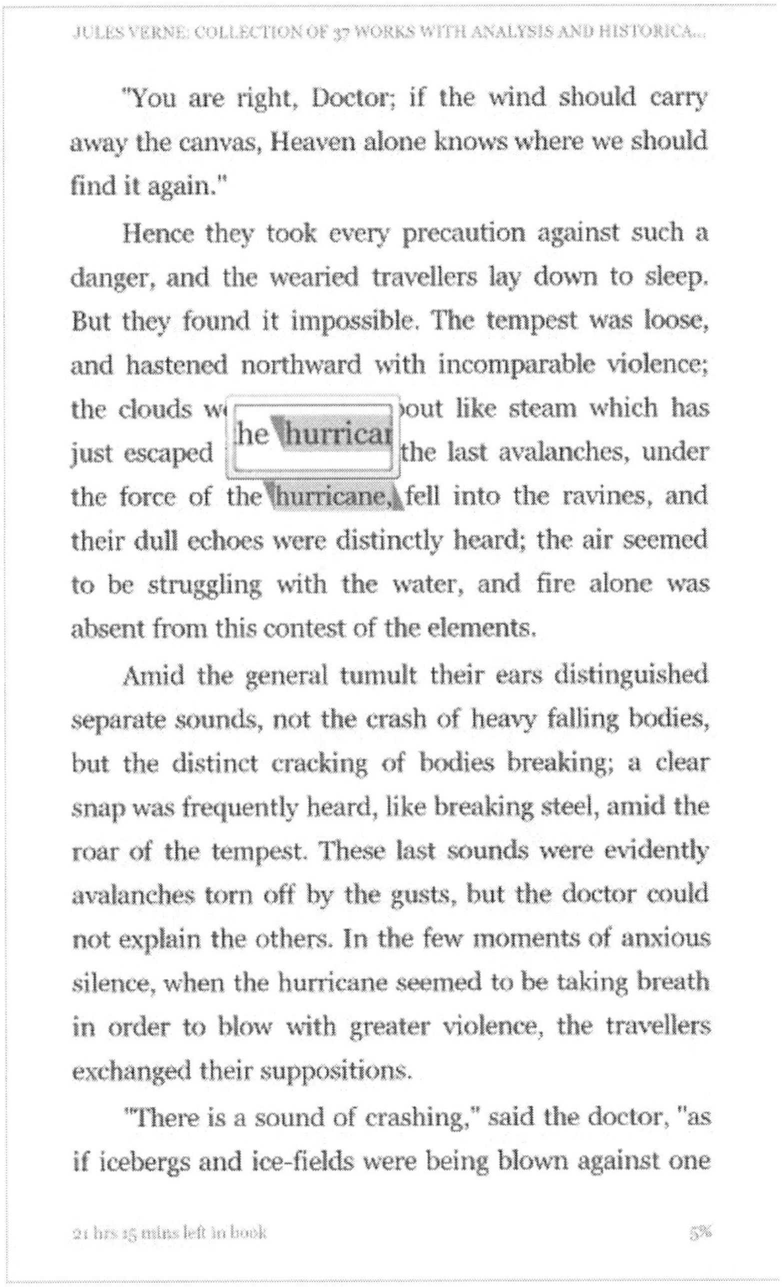

"You are right, Doctor; if the wind should carry away the canvas, Heaven alone knows where we should find it again."

Hence they took every precaution against such a danger, and the wearied travellers lay down to sleep. But they found it impossible. The tempest was loose, and hastened northward with incomparable violence; the clouds we ___ out like steam which has just escaped ___ the last avalanches, under the force of the hurricane, fell into the ravines, and their dull echoes were distinctly heard; the air seemed to be struggling with the water, and fire alone was absent from this contest of the elements.

Amid the general tumult their ears distinguished separate sounds, not the crash of heavy falling bodies, but the distinct cracking of bodies breaking; a clear snap was frequently heard, like breaking steel, amid the roar of the tempest. These last sounds were evidently avalanches torn off by the gusts, but the doctor could not explain the others. In the few moments of anxious silence, when the hurricane seemed to be taking breath in order to blow with greater violence, the travellers exchanged their suppositions.

"There is a sound of crashing," said the doctor, "as if icebergs and ice-fields were being blown against one

21 hrs 15 mins left in book   5%

Figure 4: Magnifying Glass

JULES VERNE: COLLECTION OF 37 WORKS WITH ANALYSIS AND HISTORICA...

"You are right, Doctor; if the wind should carry away the canvas, Heaven alone knows where we should find it again."

Hence they took every precaution against such a danger, and the wearied travellers lay down to sleep. But they found it impossible. The tempest was loose, and hastened northward with incomparable violence; the clouds were whirling about like steam which has just escaped from a boiler; the last avalanches, under the force of the hurricane, fell into the ravines, and their dull echoes were distinctly heard; the air seemed to be struggling with the water, and fire alone was

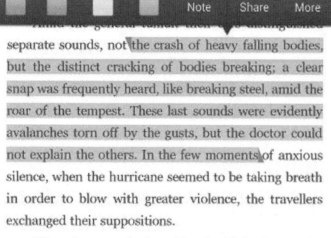

separate sounds, not the crash of heavy falling bodies, but the distinct cracking of bodies breaking; a clear snap was frequently heard, like breaking steel, amid the roar of the tempest. These last sounds were evidently avalanches torn off by the gusts, but the doctor could not explain the others. In the few moments of anxious silence, when the hurricane seemed to be taking breath in order to blow with greater violence, the travellers exchanged their suppositions.

"There is a sound of crashing," said the doctor, "as if icebergs and ice-fields were being blown against one

21 hrs 15 mins left in book   5%

Figure 5: Text Menu

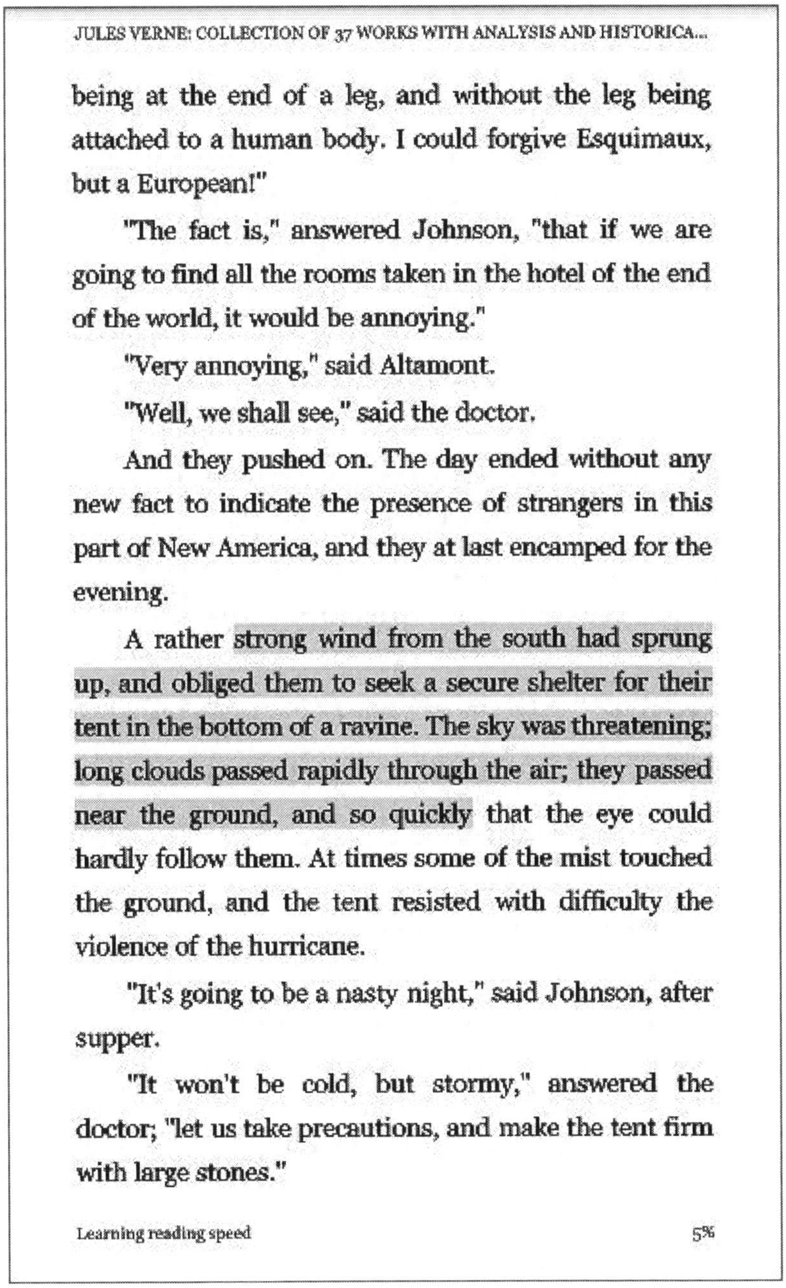

JULES VERNE: COLLECTION OF 37 WORKS WITH ANALYSIS AND HISTORICA...

being at the end of a leg, and without the leg being attached to a human body. I could forgive Esquimaux, but a European!"

"The fact is," answered Johnson, "that if we are going to find all the rooms taken in the hotel of the end of the world, it would be annoying."

"Very annoying," said Altamont.

"Well, we shall see," said the doctor.

And they pushed on. The day ended without any new fact to indicate the presence of strangers in this part of New America, and they at last encamped for the evening.

A rather strong wind from the south had sprung up, and obliged them to seek a secure shelter for their tent in the bottom of a ravine. The sky was threatening; long clouds passed rapidly through the air; they passed near the ground, and so quickly that the eye could hardly follow them. At times some of the mist touched the ground, and the tent resisted with difficulty the violence of the hurricane.

"It's going to be a nasty night," said Johnson, after supper.

"It won't be cold, but stormy," answered the doctor; "let us take precautions, and make the tent firm with large stones."

Learning reading speed   5%

Figure 6: Highlighted Phrase

4. Making a Note

While reading an eBook or periodical, notes can be added. To add a note:

1. Touch and hold a single word until the magnifying glass appears. The location where the note will be added is selected.
2. Release the screen. The Text menu appears.
3. Touch **Note**. The virtual keyboard appears at the bottom of the screen. Enter a note and touch the [Save] button. A note is added and a 🗎 icon appears next to the word. The word is also highlighted.

To remove a note:

1. Touch the 🗎 icon that corresponds to the note that you wish to remove. The Note options appear.
2. Touch **Delete**. A confirmation dialog appears.
3. Touch **Delete** again. The note is removed.

Note: Refer to "Viewing Your Notes, Highlights, and Bookmarks" *on page 59 to learn how to view your list of notes.*

5. Adding a Bookmark

While reading an eBook or periodical, the media can be bookmarked in order to quickly find the same location in the future. To add a bookmark, touch the upper right-hand corner of the screen.

A ▮ appears in the upper right-hand corner corner of the screen to indicate that the page is bookmarked, as shown in **Figure 7**.

Note: Refer to "Viewing Your Notes, Highlights, and Bookmarks" *on page 58 to learn how to view your list of bookmarks.*

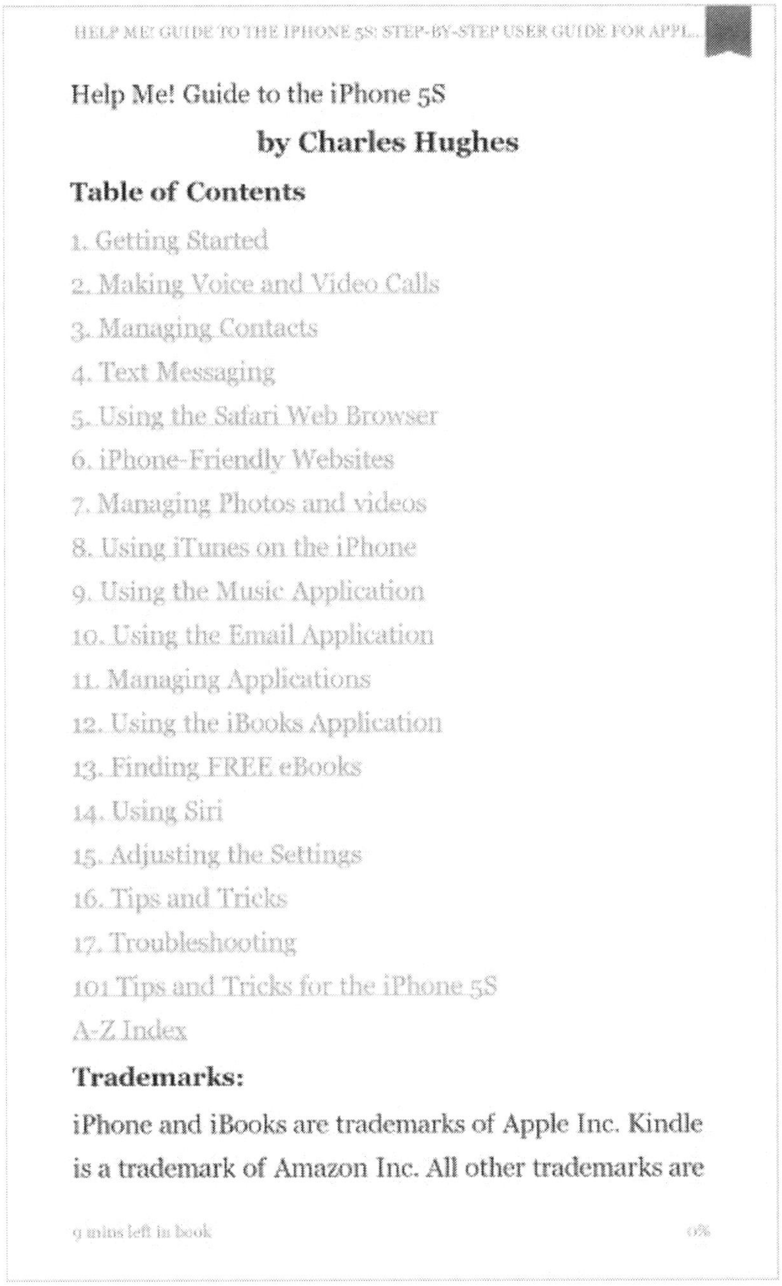

HELP ME! GUIDE TO THE IPHONE 5S: STEP-BY-STEP USER GUIDE FOR APPL...

Help Me! Guide to the iPhone 5S

by Charles Hughes

Table of Contents

Trademarks:

iPhone and iBooks are trademarks of Apple Inc. Kindle is a trademark of Amazon Inc. All other trademarks are

9 mins left in book   0%

Figure 7: Bookmarked Page

6. Viewing Your Notes, Highlights, and Bookmarks

While reading an eBook or periodical, you may view a list of all of your bookmarks, notes, and highlights in order to navigate to each directly. To view a list of your bookmarks, notes, and highlights:

1. Touch anywhere on the screen (as long as it is not a link). The eBook options appear at the top of the screen, as shown in **Figure 8**.
2. Touch **Notes**. The My Notes & Marks screen appears, as shown in **Figure 9**. Alternatively, touch **Bookmarks** to view a list of bookmarks, as shown in **Figure 10**.
3. Touch an item in the list. The Kindle Fire HDX navigates to its location. Alternatively, touch the button at the bottom of the screen to resume reading where you left off.

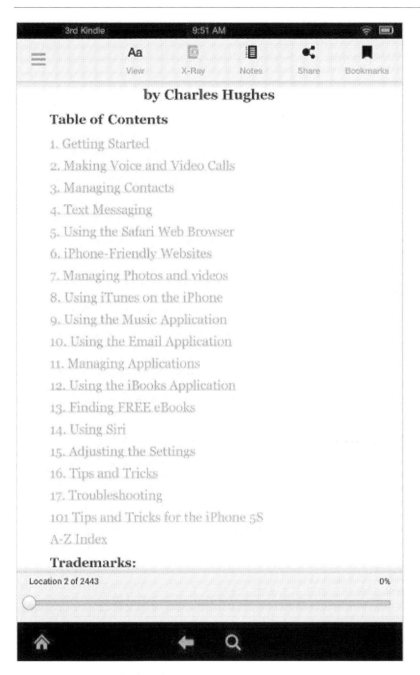

Figure 8: eBook Options

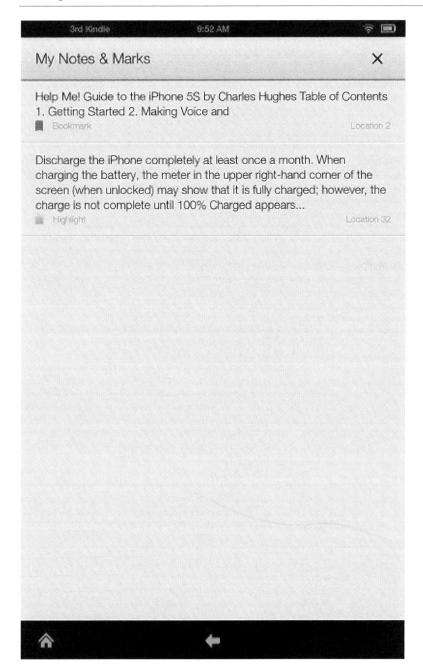

Figure 9: My Notes & Marks Screen

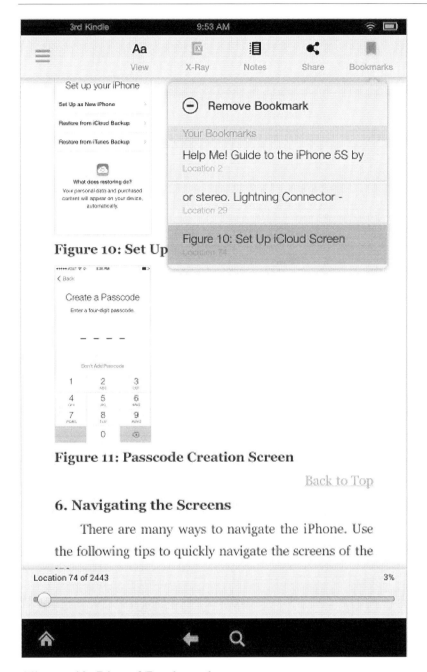

Figure 11: Passcode Creation Screen

Back to Top

6. Navigating the Screens

There are many ways to navigate the iPhone. Use the following tips to quickly navigate the screens of the

Figure 10: List of Bookmarks

7. Changing the Font Size

While reading an eBook, the size of the font can be changed. To change the font size:

1. Touch anywhere on the screen (as long as it is not a link). The eBook options appear at the top of the screen.
2. Touch **Aa** at the top of the screen. The Font menu appears, as outlined in **Figure 11**.
3. Touch the [Aa] icon to increase the font size or touch the [Aa] icon to decrease it. The font size is changed. Touch anywhere outside of the Font menu to return to reading where you left off.

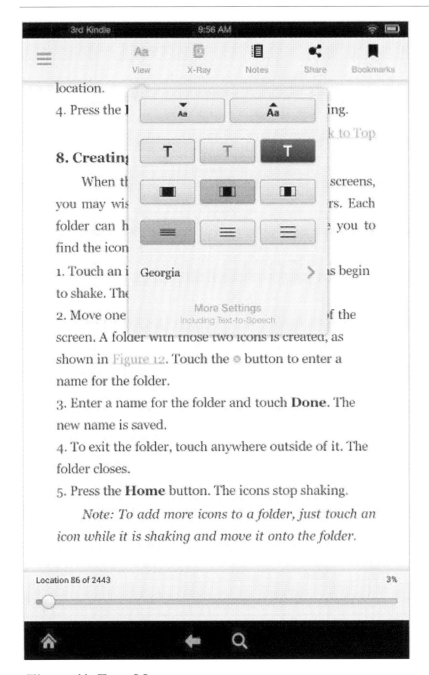

location.

4. Press the **I** ing.

k to Top

8. Creating

When th screens,
you may wis rs. Each
folder can h you to
find the icon

1. Touch an i s begin
to shake. The

2. Move one f the
screen. A folder with those two icons is created, as
shown in Figure 12. Touch the ⊙ button to enter a
name for the folder.

3. Enter a name for the folder and touch **Done**. The
new name is saved.

4. To exit the folder, touch anywhere outside of it. The
folder closes.

5. Press the **Home** button. The icons stop shaking.

*Note: To add more icons to a folder, just touch an
icon while it is shaking and move it onto the folder.*

Figure 11: Font Menu

8. Changing the Font Style

While reading an eBook, the type of font displayed can be changed. To change the font style:

1. Touch anywhere on the screen (as long as it is not a link). The eBook options appear at the top of the screen.
2. Touch **Aa** at the top of the screen. The Font menu appears.
3. Touch **Georgia**. The Font Style menu appears. Touch the menu and move your finger up or down to scroll through the available styles.
4. Touch a style in the list. The font style is changed. Touch anywhere outside of the Font Style menu to return to reading where you left off.

9. Changing the Color Mode

While reading an eBook, you may change the Color mode. The available options are black on white (the default), white on black, and brown on sepia. To change the Color mode:

1. Touch anywhere on the screen (as long as it is not a link). The eBook options appear at the top of the screen.
2. Touch **Aa** at the top of the screen. The Font menu appears.
3. Touch the [T] button, [T] button, or [T] (Sepia) button. The new Color mode is applied. Touch anywhere outside of the Font menu to return to reading where you left off.

10. Changing the Screen Orientation

While reading an eBook, the screen can be rotated. To change the screen orientation, rotate the Kindle to the left or right. If the Kindle is upside down, the screen will still orient correctly. If the screen does not rotate, refer to *"Screen does not rotate"* on page 256 to learn how to resolve the problem.

11. Searching an eBook

You may search an eBook for a particular word or phrase. To search an eBook:

1. Touch anywhere on the screen (as long as it is not a link). The eBook menu appears at the bottom of the screen.
2. Touch the button at the bottom of the screen. The Search field appears at the top of the screen.
3. Enter a search word or phrase and touch **Go**. A list of matching results appears, as shown in **Figure 12**. Touch a search result to navigate to its location.

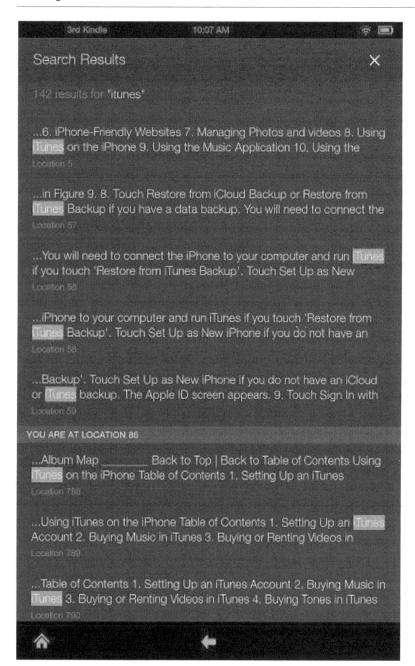

Figure 12: List of Matching Results

12. Sharing a Passage with Facebook Friends or Twitter Followers

You may share passages contained in eBooks with your friends on Facebook. To share a passage:

1. Touch and hold a single word until the magnifying glass appears. You may now select the text that you wish to highlight.
2. Drag your finger without letting go of the screen to select a phrase. The phrase is selected and the Text menu appears.
3. Touch **Share**. The Shared Notes & Highlights screen appears, as shown in **Figure 13**.
4. Touch the ![f] icon or the ![twitter] icon to select where the passage will be shared. A ![check] icon appears next to each selected icon. If you are not already signed in to your social networks, refer to *"Logging In to Your Facebook and Twitter Accounts"* on page 245 to learn how to log in.
5. Touch the ![Share] button. The selected passage is shared on the selected social networks.

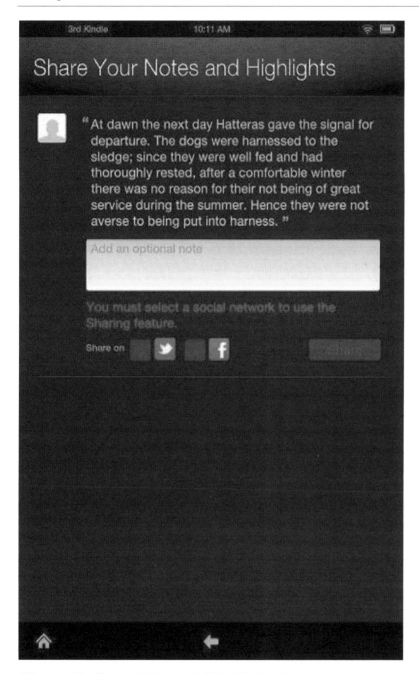

Figure 13: Shared Notes & Highlights Screen

13. Looking Up Characters or Terms in a Story

The Kindle Fire HDX has a built-in feature, called X-Ray, which allows you to look up the names and descriptions of characters and terms in a story. To look up characters or terms:

1. Touch anywhere on the screen (as long as it is not a link). The eBook options appear at the top of the screen.
2. Touch **X-Ray**. A list of characters and terms appears, as shown in **Figure 14**.
3. Touch **People** or **Terms** at the top of the screen. The corresponding list of items appears.
4. Touch a character or term in the list. The device navigates to the specified location. You can also touch **Full Wikipedia Article** when viewing a term to read more about it.

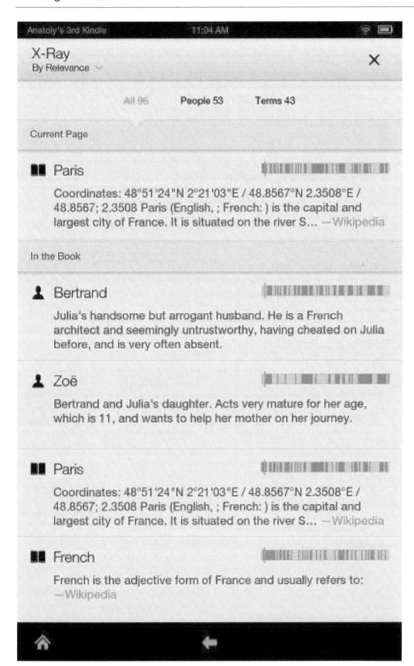

Figure 14: List of Characters and Terms

Managing and Listening to Audiobooks

Table of Contents

1. Purchasing an Audiobook

In addition to reading eBooks on the Kindle Fire HDX, you may listen to audiobooks. To purchase an audiobook:

1. Touch **Audiobooks** at the top of the library. The Audiobooks Store appears, as shown in **Figure 1**. Touch **Store** in the upper right-hand corner if you do not see the store.

2. Touch the icon at the top of the screen. The virtual keyboard appears.

3. Enter the name of an audiobook or author and touch **Go**. A list of matching audiobook results appears, as shown in **Figure 2**.

4. Touch an audiobook in the list. The Audiobook description appears, as shown in **Figure 3**.

5. Touch **Buy for $##.##**, where ##.## represents the price of the audiobook. The audiobook is purchased and downloaded to your device. The audiobook will appear as the first item in your library when you touch the button.

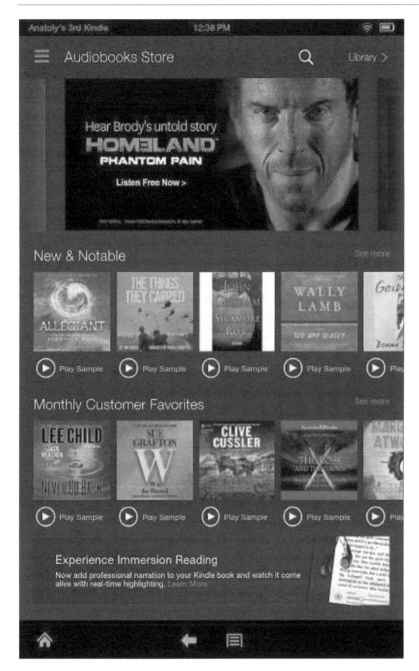

Figure 1: Audiobooks Store

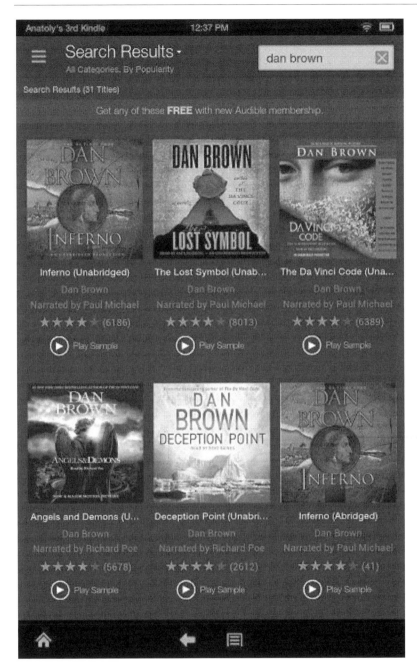

Figure 2: List of Matching Audiobook Results

Figure 3: Audiobook Description

2. Listening to an Audiobook

You may listen to audiobooks right on your Kindle Fire HDX. To listen to an audiobook:

1. Touch **Audiobooks**. The Audiobooks library appears, as shown in **Figure 4**.
2. Touch the cover of an audiobook. The audiobook appears, as shown in **Figure 5**. Touch the 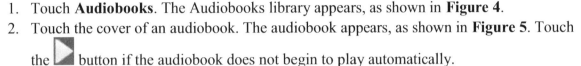 button if the audiobook does not begin to play automatically.
3. Use the following controls at the bottom of the screen while listening to an audiobook:

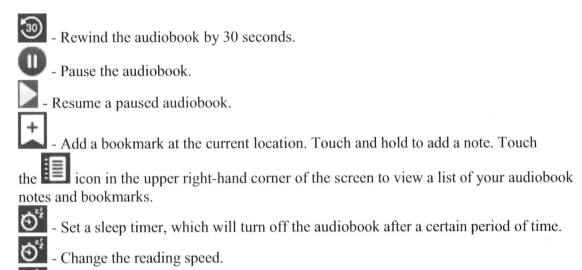 - Rewind the audiobook by 30 seconds.

- Pause the audiobook.

- Resume a paused audiobook.

- Add a bookmark at the current location. Touch and hold to add a note. Touch the icon in the upper right-hand corner of the screen to view a list of your audiobook notes and bookmarks.

- Set a sleep timer, which will turn off the audiobook after a certain period of time.

- Change the reading speed.

- Adjust the volume. You can also use the volume buttons. Refer to *"Button Layout"* on page 7 to learn where the volume buttons are located.

Figure 4: Audiobooks Library

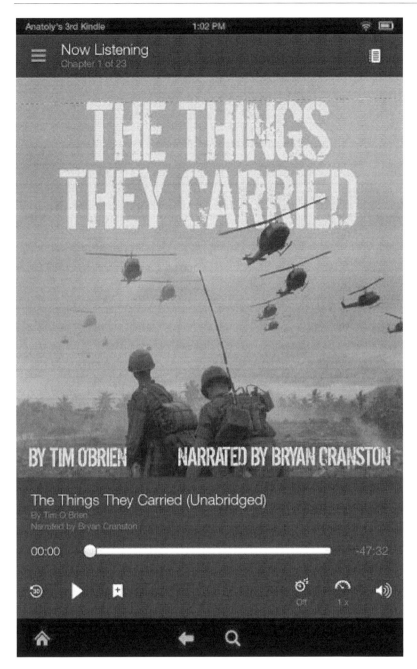

Figure 5: Audiobook

3. Navigating to a Specific Chapter in an Audiobook

To skip to a specific chapter while listening to an audiobook, touch the left edge of the screen and move your finger to the right. A list of chapters appears, as shown in **Figure 6**. Touch a chapter in the list. The audiobook skips to the selected chapter and begins to play.

Figure 6: List of Chapters

4. Reading an eBook while Listening to the Companion Audiobook

The Kindle Fire HDX allows you to listen to an audiobook while reading the companion Kindle eBook. Make sure that you own both the audiobook and the companion Kindle eBook before proceeding. Refer to *"Buying an eBook on the Kindle Fire HDX"* on page 25 to learn how to purchase an eBook. Refer to *"Purchasing an Audiobook"* on page 71 to learn how to purchase an audiobook. To listen to an audiobook while reading an eBook, touch anywhere on the page (except for a link), and then touch the ▶ icon in the lower left-hand corner of the screen. The audiobook turns on, and words are highlighted in gray as they are read. Refer to *"Reading eBooks and Periodicals"* on page 48 to learn more about eBooks.

5. Archiving and Restoring an Audiobook

An audiobook can be removed from your Kindle Fire HDX and placed in the Amazon Cloud where it does not take up space on your device. An archived audiobook is retrievable using the wireless connection. To archive an audiobook:

1. Touch **Audiobooks**. The Audiobooks library appears.
2. Touch and hold the audiobook that you wish archive. The item menu appears, as shown in **Figure 7**.
3. Touch **Remove from Device**. The selected audiobook is archived. You can always download the audiobook back to your device by touching **Cloud** at the top of the Audiobook library, and then touching the cover of the audiobook.

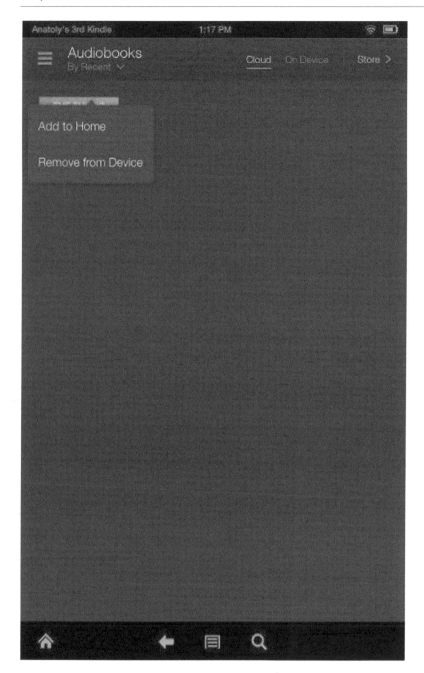

Figure 7: Item Menu

Managing Movies and TV Shows

Table of Contents

1. Browsing Movies and TV Shows in the Video Store

You can browse the Amazon library of movies and TV shows right on your Kindle Fire HDX. To browse movies and TV shows:

1. Touch **Videos** at the top of the Library. The Video store opens, as shown in **Figure 1**. Touch **Store** in the upper right-hand corner if you do not see the store.

2. Touch the [icon] icon at the top of the screen. The virtual keyboard appears.

3. Enter the name of a movie or TV show. A list of matching results appears, as shown in **Figure 2**. You can also browse by category by touching the left edge of the screen and sliding your finger to the right.

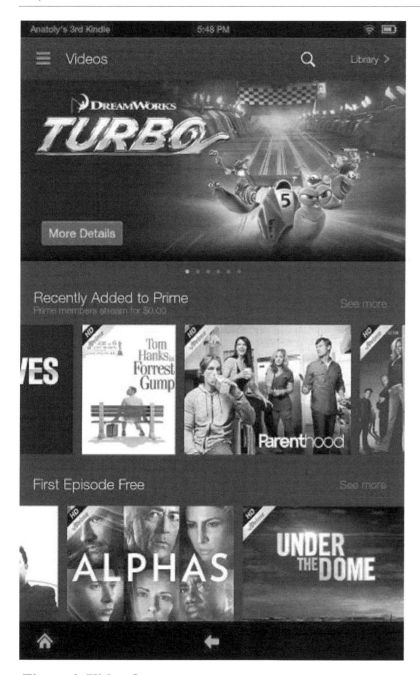

Figure 1: Video Store

Figure 2: List of Matching Results

2. Buying or Renting a Movie

You can purchase or rent movies from the Amazon library using your Kindle Fire HDX. To buy or rent a movie:

1. Find the movie that you wish to buy or rent. Refer to *"Browsing Movies and TV Shows in the Video Store"* on page 81 to learn how.
2. Touch the movie thumbnail. The Movie description appears, as shown in **Figure 3**.
3. Touch **Rent** or **Buy**. The orange button turns green.
4. Touch **Rent** or **Buy** again. The movie is purchased and downloaded to your Kindle Fire HDX. Touch **Download** to load the movie onto your Kindle Fire HDX or **Watch Now** to stream it using a Wi-Fi connection.

Note: When renting a movie, you have 30 days to begin to watch it, with the movie expiring 48 hours after you touch 'Watch Now' or 'Download'. Downloading a movie to the Kindle Fire HDX allows you to watch it while not connected to the internet. However, you may only download the movie to one device at a time and cannot stream it on another device registered to your Amazon account while it is loaded onto the Kindle Fire HDX.

Figure 3: Movie Description

3. Buying or Renting a TV Show

You can purchase or rent TV shows from the Amazon library using your Kindle Fire HDX. To buy or rent a TV show:

1. Find the TV show you wish to buy or rent. Refer to *"Browsing Movies and TV Shows in the Video Store"* on page 81 to learn how.
2. Touch the movie thumbnail. The TV Show description and a list of episodes appear, as shown in **Figure 4**.
3. Touch the **Buy Episode** or **Buy Season** to purchase the corresponding item. The orange 'Buy' button turns green.
4. Touch **Buy Episode** or **Buy Season** again. The episode or season is purchased. Touch **Watch** to stream the TV show.

Note: Downloading a TV show to the Kindle Fire HDX allows you to watch it while not connected to the internet. However, you may only download the TV show to one device at a time and cannot stream it on another device registered to your Amazon account while it is loaded onto the Kindle Fire HDX.

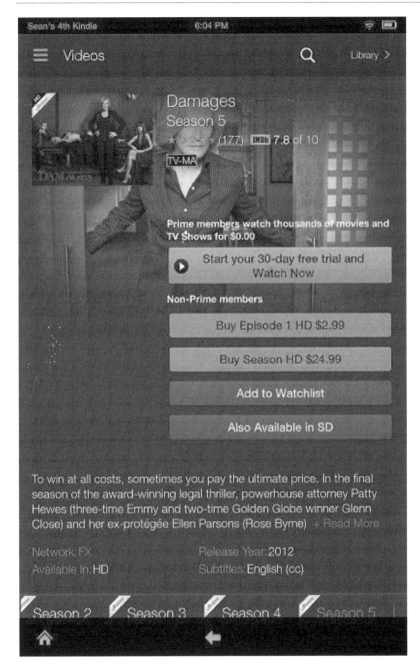

Figure 4: TV Show Description

4. Playing a Movie or TV Show

The Kindle Fire HDX can play movies and TV shows from the library. To play a movie or TV show:

1. Touch **Videos** at the top of the Library. The Video store opens.
2. Touch **Library** in the upper right-hand corner of the screen. The Video library opens, as shown in **Figure 5**.
3. Touch **Movies** or **TV**. The corresponding library opens.
4. Touch a video thumbnail. The video description appears, as shown in **Figure 6**.
5. Touch **Watch Now**. The video begins to play.
6. Use the following tips to control the playback of a video:

   - **Controlling the Volume** - Use the volume buttons to control the volume. Refer to *"Button Layout"* on page 7 to learn where the volume buttons are located.
   - **Pausing and Resuming the Video** - Touch the screen anywhere. The Video controls appear, as shown in **Figure 7**. Touch the ![pause] button. The video is paused. Touch the ![play] button. Video playback resumes.
   - **Rewinding by Ten Seconds** - Touch the screen anywhere. The Video controls appear. Touch the ![rewind 10] button. The video rewinds by ten seconds and resumes playing. You can also rewind while the movie is paused. When you touch the ![play] button, the movie will resume from the new location.
   - **Navigating to a Specific Location** - Touch the screen anywhere. The Video controls appear. Touch the ![slider] on the ▬▬▬▬▬●▬▬▬▬▬ bar and drag it to the desired location. The video skips to the location and continues to play.

Note: If a video has not downloaded or buffered completely, you will not be able to navigate to a location that has not yet finished loading.

Figure 5: Video Library

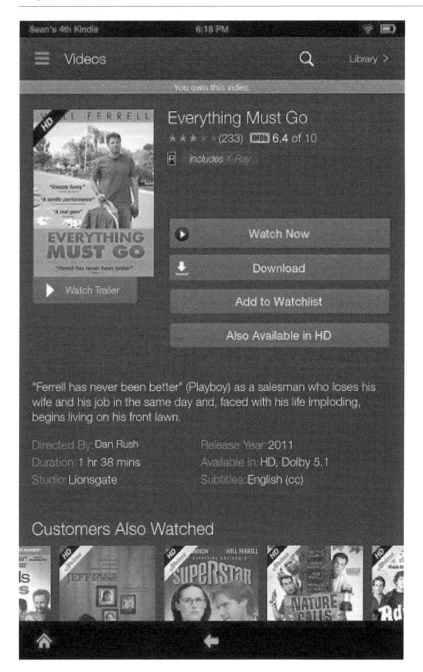

Figure 6: Video Description

Figure 7: Video Controls

5. Using X-Ray for Movies

While watching a movie, you can use X-Ray to look up the names of the actors that are in the current scene, as well as the song that is currently playing. To use X-Ray for movies, touch the screen anywhere while a movie is playing. A list of actors and the current song, if any, appears on the left-hand side of the screen. Touch the name of an actor to look up his or her biography and filmography. Touch the name of the song to view a list of all songs that can be heard in the movie. Touch **Jump to Scene** if you wish to skip to a scene where a particular song is played.

6. Archiving Movies and TV Shows

Any movies or TV shows that are stored on your Kindle Fire HDX can be archived and stored in the Amazon Cloud where they do not take up space on your device. To archive movies and TV shows:

1. Touch **Videos** at the top of the Library. The Video store opens.
2. Touch **Library** in the upper right-hand corner of the screen. The Video library opens.
3. Touch **Movies** or **TV** to find the video that you wish to archive. The corresponding video library opens.
4. Touch and hold a video thumbnail. The Video menu appears.
5. Touch **Delete Download**. The video is archived in the Amazon Cloud.

7. Importing Movies from an Outside Source Using Your PC or Mac

Movies that you have purchased or downloaded elsewhere can be imported to the Kindle Fire HDX. Supported video formats include MP4, 3GP, and VP8. To import movies:

1. Connect the Kindle Fire HDX to your computer using the provided USB cable.
2. Open **My Computer** on a PC and double-click the 'KINDLE' removable drive. On a Mac, you will need to download the Android File Transfer utility, which can be downloaded at **http://www.android.com/filetransfer/**. The Kindle Folders open on a PC, as shown in **Figure 8**, or on a Mac, as shown in **Figure 9**.
3. Double-click the **Movies** folder. The Video folder opens.
4. Drag and drop a video into the Video folder. The video is copied and will appear in the Photos application on your Kindle Fire HDX, given that it is of the correct format.

Note: To access the transferred video, touch **Photos** *at the top of the screen, touch* **All**, *and then touch* **Videos**.

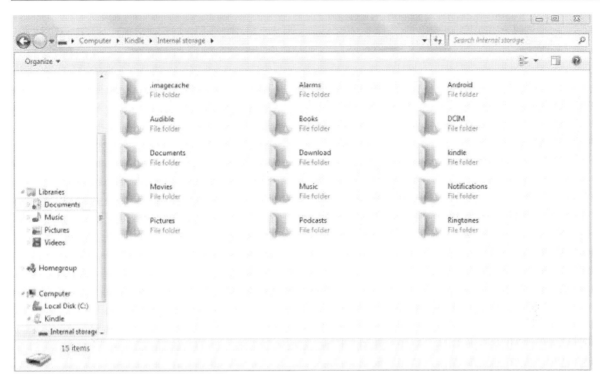

Figure 8: Kindle Folders on a PC

Figure 9: Kindle Folders on a Mac

Managing Music

Table of Contents

1. Browsing Music

You can browse the Amazon music store right on your Kindle Fire HDX. To browse music:

1. Touch **Music** at the top of the Library. The Music library appears, as shown in **Figure 1**.
2. Touch **Store** in the upper right-hand corner of the screen. The Music store opens, as shown in **Figure 2**.
3. Touch the icon at the top of the screen. The virtual keyboard appears.
4. Enter the name of an artist, song, or album, and touch the button. A list of matching results appears, as shown in **Figure 3**.
5. Touch a result in the list. The music description appears, as shown in **Figure 4** (artist description). You can also touch an artist's name to see all available albums by that artist. Touch the button next to a song to preview it.

Note: Refer to "Buying a Song or Album" *on page 99 to learn how to purchase a song or album.*

Figure 1: Music Library

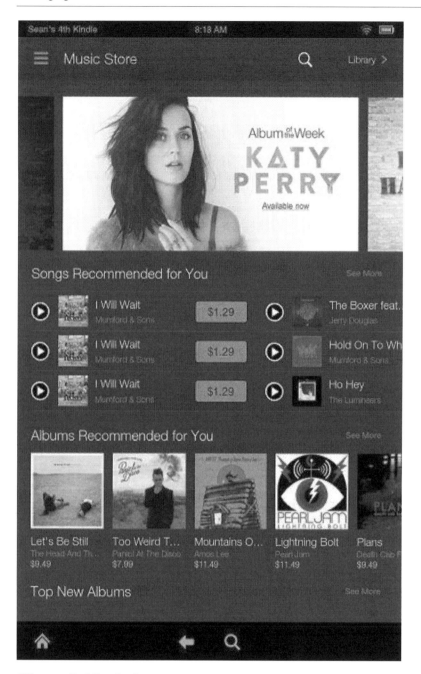

Figure 2: Music Store

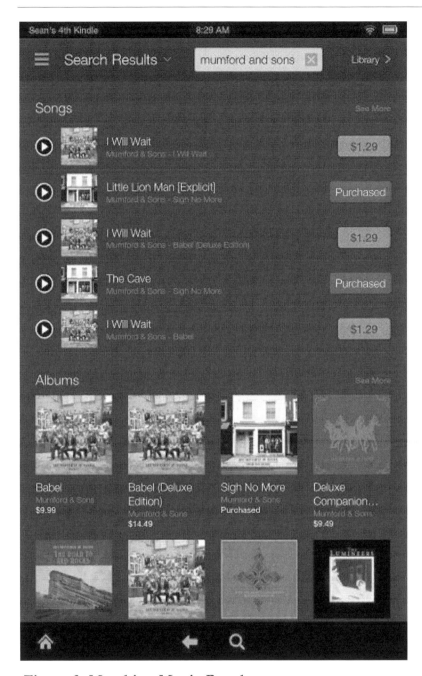

Figure 3: Matching Music Results

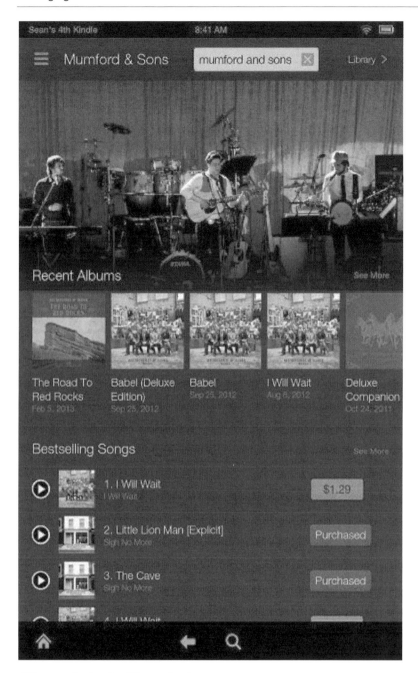

Figure 4: Artist Description

2. Buying a Song or Album

You can purchase music from the Amazon store using your Kindle Fire HDX. To buy a song or album:

1. Find the album containing the song you wish to download. Refer to *"Browsing Music"* on page 94 to learn how.
2. Touch the name of the album. The list of songs appears, as shown in **Figure 5**. Touch the ▶ button next to a song to preview it.
3. Touch the price of a song or album. The **Buy** button appears.
4. Touch the **Buy** button. The song or album is purchased and stored in your Amazon Cloud.
5. Touch **Play Now** to stream the song from your cloud.

Note: Refer to "Tips and Tricks" *on page 248 to learn how to set the Kindle Fire HDX to automatically download a song to the cloud or device when buying music.*

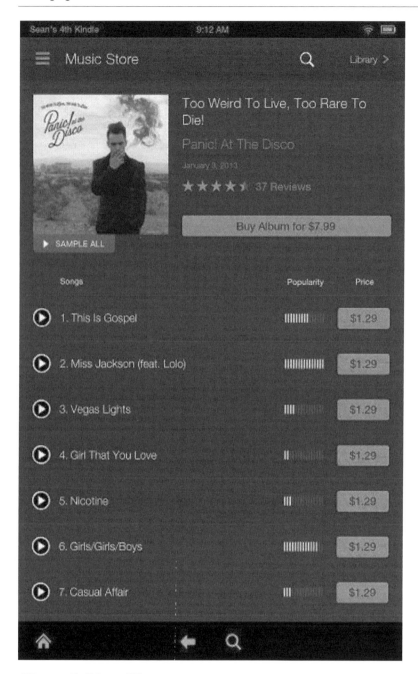

Figure 5: List of Songs

3. Playing a Song

You can play music using your Kindle Fire HDX. To play a song:

1. Touch **Music** at the top of the Library. The Music library appears.
2. Touch **Cloud** or **Device**, depending on where your music is stored. The corresponding storage location opens.
3. Touch a category at the top of the music list (**Playlists**, **Artists**, etc.). The corresponding category appears.
4. Touch an artist to view the corresponding albums and touch an album to view the corresponding songs. Touch a song. The song begins to play, as shown in **Figure 6**.

Note: To add an entire artist or album to the 'Now Playing' list, touch and hold the corresponding item and touch **Add to Playlist**.

Figure 6: Song Playing

4. Controlling the Music

While a song is playing, touch one of the following buttons to perform the associated action:

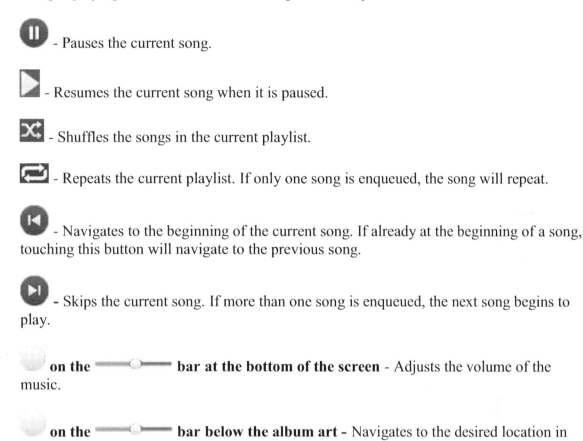

 - Pauses the current song.

 - Resumes the current song when it is paused.

 - Shuffles the songs in the current playlist.

 - Repeats the current playlist. If only one song is enqueued, the song will repeat.

 - Navigates to the beginning of the current song. If already at the beginning of a song, touching this button will navigate to the previous song.

 - Skips the current song. If more than one song is enqueued, the next song begins to play.

 on the ═══○══ **bar at the bottom of the screen** - Adjusts the volume of the music.

 on the ═══○══ **bar below the album art -** Navigates to the desired location in the current song.

 (upper left-hand corner) - Opens the music library. Touch the name of the song at the bottom of the screen to return to the 'Now Playing' screen at any time.

Note: Refer to "Tips and Tricks" *on page 248* *to learn how to make music controls appear on the Lock screen.*

5. Creating and Editing a Playlist

Playlists can be created and edited right on the Kindle Fire HDX. You can only create a playlist with the music on your device.

To create a playlist:

1. Touch **Music** at the top of the Library. The Music library appears.
2. Touch **On Device** at the top of the screen. The music stored on your device appears.
3. Touch the left edge of the screen and slide your finger to the right. The Music menu appears, as shown in **Figure 7**.
4. Touch **Playlists**. The existing playlists appear, as shown in **Figure 8**.
5. Touch the ![+] icon at the top of the screen. The New Playlist window appears, as shown in **Figure 9**.
6. Enter a name for the new playlist and touch **Save**. The new playlist is created and a list of songs appears.
7. Touch the ![+] button next to a song. The song is added to the playlist.
8. Touch the ![Done] button in the upper right-hand corner of the screen. The playlist is saved.

To edit a playlist:

1. Follow steps 1-3 above. The existing playlists appear.
2. Touch a playlist. The songs within the playlist appear.
3. Touch **Edit**. The Playlist Editing screen appears, as shown in **Figure 10**.
4. Use the following tips to edit a playlist:

   - Touch the ![−] button to the right of a song to remove it from the playlist.
   - Touch **Add Songs** at the top of the screen to add a song to the playlist. A list of songs appears. Touch the ![+] button next to a song to add it to the playlist.
   - Touch the ![icon] icon to the left of a song and drag it up or down to change the order of the songs.
   - Touch **Rename** to rename the playlist.

Note: You can only create a playlist with music downloaded to your device.

Figure 7: Music Menu

Figure 8: Existing Playlists

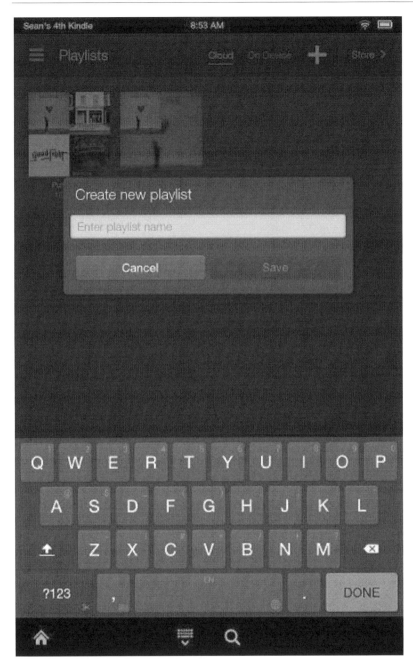

Figure 9: New Playlist Window

Figure 10: Playlist Editing Screen

6. Archiving Music

Any music that is stored on your Kindle Fire HDX can be removed from your device and stored in the Amazon Cloud. To archive music:

1. Touch **Music** at the top of the Library. The Music library appears.
2. Touch **On Device**. The music stored on your device appears.
3. Touch and hold an artist, album, or song. The Music Management options appear, as shown in **Figure 11**.
4. Touch **Remove from device**. The selected music is removed from your device and stored in the Cloud.

Note: Any music purchased from the Amazon store is automatically stored in the Amazon cloud. You will not lose your music when you remove it from your device.

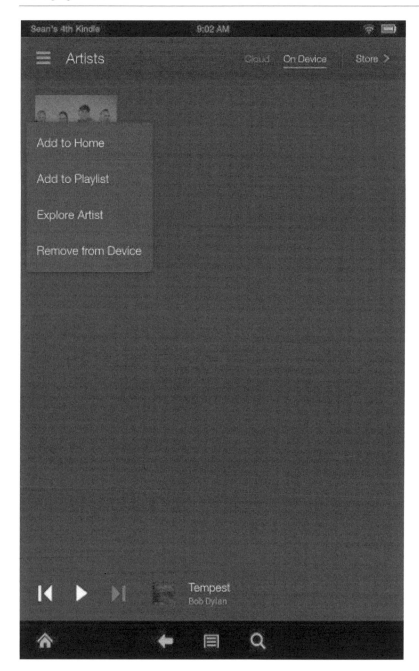

Figure 11: Music Management Options

7. Importing Music from an Outside Source Using Your PC or Mac

Music that you have purchased or downloaded elsewhere can be imported to the Kindle Fire HDX. Supported audio formats include non-DRM AAC, MP3, OGG, WAV, and MP4. To import music:

1. Connect the Kindle Fire HDX to your computer using the provided USB cable. The USB Connected screen appears.
2. Open **My Computer** on a PC and double-click the 'KINDLE' removable drive. On a Mac, you will need to download the Android File Transfer utility, which can be found at **http://www.android.com/filetransfer/**. The Kindle Folders open on a PC, as shown in **Figure 12**, or on a Mac, as shown in **Figure 13**.
3. Double-click the **Music** folder. The Music folder opens.
4. Drag and drop a song or folder of music into the Video folder. The music is copied and will appear in the Music library.

Note: You can also transfer any music from the Kindle Fire HDX to your computer by dragging and dropping it from the Music folder to your computer. Even songs purchased in the Amazon Music Store can be transferred to your computer.

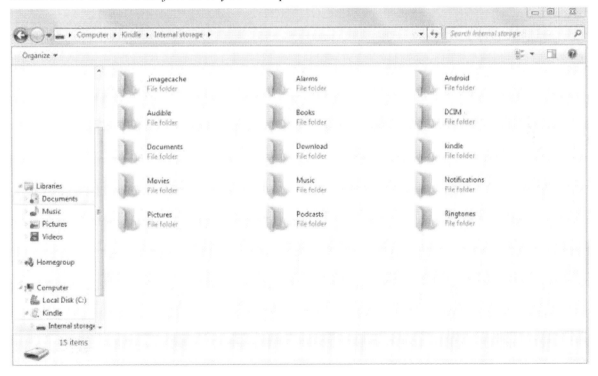

Figure 12: Kindle Folders on a PC

Figure 13: Kindle Folders on a Mac

Managing Email

Table of Contents

1. Adding an Email Account to the Kindle Fire HDX

Before you can send and receive email using the Email application, you must add an email account to the device. The first time that you open the email application, the device allows you to add an account. To add an email account:

1. Touch **Apps** at the top of the Library. The Apps Library appears, as shown in **Figure 1**.
2. Touch the icon. The Email application opens, and the Add Account screen appears, as shown in **Figure 2**.
3. Enter your email address and touch **Done**. The password field appears. If you have a Google account, the Google Account screen appears, where you can enter your password.
4. Enter your password and touch **Go**. Your email account is added to the Kindle Fire HDX. You will need to touch **Accept** on the following screen if you are adding a Google account.
5. Touch **Go to Inbox**. Your inbox appears.

Figure 1: Apps Library

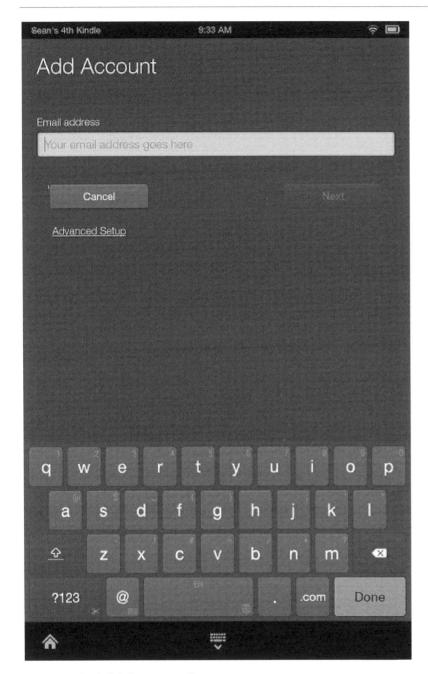

Figure 2: Add Account Screen

2. Reading Email

You can read the email in your Email inbox on the Kindle Fire HDX. To read email:

1. Touch the icon. The Email application opens, and the Inbox appears, as shown in **Figure 3**.
2. Touch an email in the list. The email opens, as shown in **Figure 4**.
3. Touch the email anywhere and slide your finger to the left or right. The previous or next email appears, respectively.
4. Touch the icon in the upper left-hand corner of the screen. The Inbox appears.

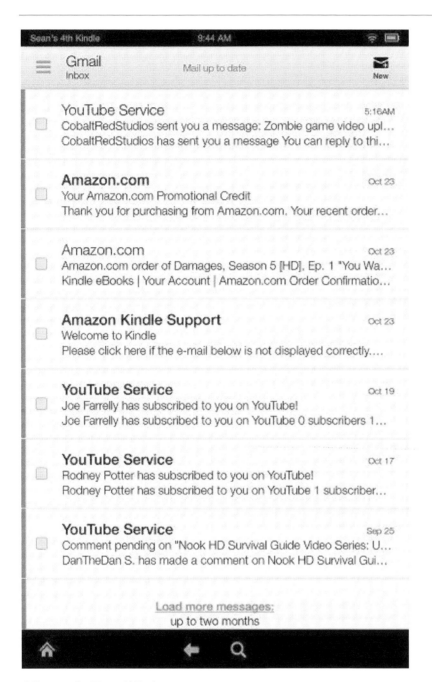

Figure 3: Email Inbox

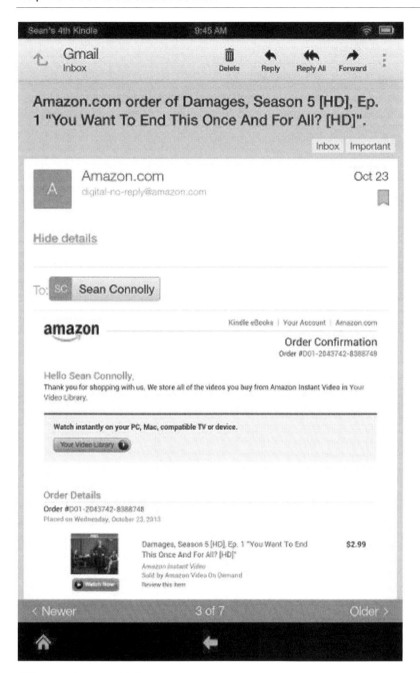

Figure 4: Email Open

3. Writing an Email

Compose email directly from the Kindle Fire HDX using your email account. To write an email:

1. Touch the icon. The Email application opens.
2. Touch the icon in the upper right-hand corner of the screen. The Compose screen appears, as shown in **Figure 5**.
3. Enter the recipient's email address in the 'To:' field. Enter an optional subject. Touch the white space below 'Subject' and enter your message.
4. Touch the button in the upper right-hand corner of the screen. The email is sent.

Figure 5: Compose Screen

4. Replying to and Forwarding Emails

After receiving an email in your Gmail inbox, a reply can be sent or the email can be forwarded. To reply to or forward an email:

1. Touch the icon. The Email application opens.
2. Touch the email to which you wish to reply or that you wish to forward. The email opens.
3. Touch one of the following icons at the top of the screen to reply to or forward an email, as outlined in **Figure 6**:

    - Creates a reply to the sender of the email.

    - Creates a reply to the sender of the email, as well as anyone else who received the same email.

    - Creates a new email with the content of the original email copied into it. You will need to enter the recipient's email address.

4. Enter the message in the white space below 'Subject'.

5. Touch the button in the upper right-hand corner of the screen. The email is sent.

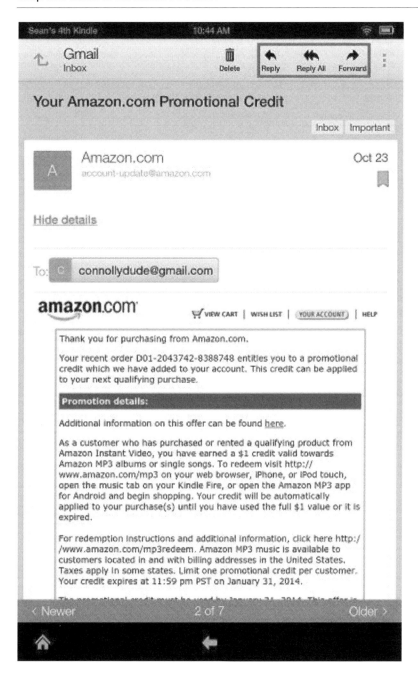

Figure 6: Reply and Forward Icons Outlined

5. Deleting Emails

Emails can be deleted to free up room in your Inbox. To delete an email:

1. Touch the ▨ icon. The Email application opens.

2. Touch the ▢ box to the left of each email that you wish to delete. A ☑ box appears next to each selected email.

3. Touch the 🗑 icon at the top of the screen. The selected emails are deleted.

6. Moving an Email to a Different Folder

Moving emails between folders, such as 'Work' or 'Personal', can be a helpful organizational tool. To move an email to a different folder:

1. Touch the ▨ icon. The Email application opens.

2. Touch the ▢ box to the left of each email that you wish to move. A ☑ box appears next to each selected email.

3. Touch the 📁 icon at the top of the screen. A list of available folders appears, as shown in **Figure 7**.

4. Touch the name of the folder to which you wish to move the emails. An ⬤ icon appears next to the selected folder.

5. Touch **Apply**. The selected emails are moved to the folder.

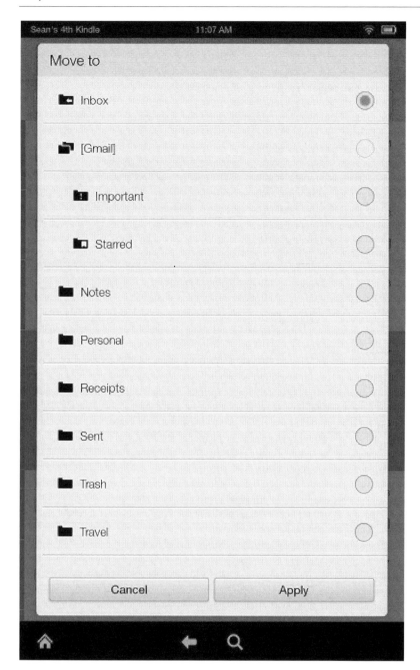

Figure 7: List of Available Folders

7. Searching the Inbox

To find a message in your inbox on the Kindle Fire HDX, use the search function, which searches email addresses, message text, and subject lines. To search the Inbox:

1. Touch the ⬜ icon. The Email application opens.
2. Touch the 🔍 icon at the bottom of the screen. 'Search messages on device' appears at the top of the screen.
3. Touch **From** to the left of the Search field and select whether to search by the sender, recipient, subject of the email, or all text, including the content of the email. The search criteria is set.
4. Enter a search word or phrase, or the name or email address of a sender. The matching results appear as you type.

*Note: Searching using the 'All' criteria will disable instant search. In this case, touch **Search** to initiate the search.*

8. Managing Email Labels

Emails can be classified according to the nature of the message, such as 'work' or 'personal'. To add labels to emails:

1. Touch the ⬜ icon. The Email application opens.
2. Touch the ⬜ box to the left of each email that you wish to label. A ☑ box appears next to each selected email.
3. Touch the ⠿ icon in the upper right-hand corner of the screen. The Inbox menu appears, as shown in **Figure 8**.
4. Touch **Label**. A list of available labels appears, as shown in **Figure 9**.
5. Touch as many labels as you wish to apply to the message. An orange ☑ mark appears next to each selected label.
6. Touch **Apply** at the bottom of the screen. The selected labels are applied to the email.

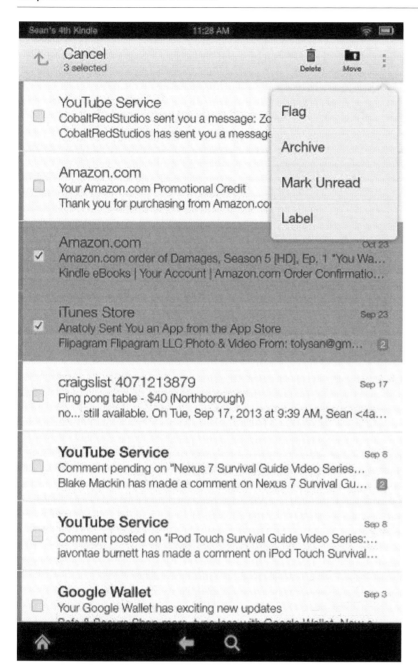

Figure 8: Inbox Menu

Figure 9: List of Available Labels

Managing Photos and Videos

Table of Contents

1. Taking a Picture

The Kindle Fire HDX has a built-in front-facing, 1.2 megapixel camera. If you have the 8.9" model, you also have a rear-facing 8 megapixel camera. To take a picture:

1. Touch **Apps** at the top of the Library. The Apps library appears, as shown in **Figure 1**.

2. Touch the icon. The camera turns on, as shown in **Figure 2**.

3. Touch the button. The camera takes a picture and stores it in the 'Camera Roll' photo album. Refer to *"Browsing Pictures"* on page 131 to learn how to view your captured photos.

Figure 1: Apps Library

Figure 2: Camera Turned On

2. Capturing a Video

The Kindle Fire HDX has a built-in camcorder that can capture HD video. To capture a video:

1. Touch **Apps** at the top of the Library. The Apps library appears.

2. Touch the ⊚ icon. The camera turns on.

3. Touch the ◉ icon. The camcorder turns on.

4. Touch the ● button. The camcorder starts to record.

5. Touch the ◉ button. The camcorder stops recording and the video is stored in the 'Camera Roll' album.

3. Browsing Pictures

You can browse captured or saved photos using the Photos application. To view the images stored on your device:

1. Touch **Photos** at the top of the library. The first time that the Photos application opens, the device will offer various services that allow you to add pictures from other devices. You may skip this for now, if you like, by touching the X in the upper right-hand corner of the screen. The thumbnails of the pictures on your device appear, as shown in **Figure 3**.
2. Touch a photo. The photo appears in full-screen mode.
3. Touch the photo with two fingers spread apart and move them together. The photo thumbnails reappear.
4. Touch the edge of the screen and move your finger to the right. A list of available photo albums appears, as shown in **Figure 4**. Touch a photo album to open it.

Figure 3: Picture Thumbnails

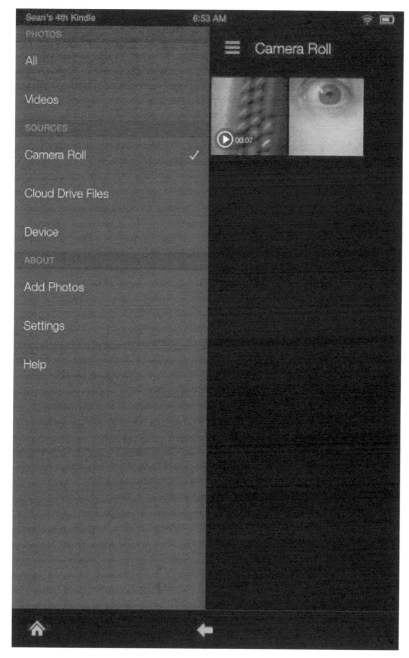

Figure 4: Available Photo Albums

4. Enhancing Pictures and Applying Special Effects

You may enhance a picture using various effects. To enhance a picture:

1. Touch **Photos** at the top of the library. The thumbnails of the pictures on your device appear.
2. Touch and hold the picture that you wish to edit. The Picture options appear, as shown in **Figure 5**.
3. Touch **Edit**. The Picture Editing screen appears, as shown in **Figure 6**.
4. Touch one of the following icons at the bottom of the screen, and then touch **Apply** in the upper right-hand corner of the screen to apply the corresponding enhancement:

- Improve the quality of the photo. Touch **Hi-Def**, **Illuminate**, or **Color Fix** to apply the corresponding enhancement.

- Remove a red eye from the photo. Touch each red eye to correct it.

- Applies a color effect, similar to Sepia or Grayscale.

- Adds clip art stickers to the picture.

- Add text on top of the picture.

- Creates a meme for a social network, allowing you to edit pre-defined text boxes at the top and bottom of the picture.

- Allows you to draw on the picture. You will be able to select the color and thickness of the paintbrush.

- Adjusts the brightness of the photo.

- Adjusts the contrast of the picture.

- Adjusts the color saturation. The higher the saturation, the more color there will be in the picture.

- Adjusts the amount of warm or cool colors in the picture. Warm colors are associated with daylight or a sunset, whereas cool colors are associated with a gray or overcast day.

 - Adjusts specific parts of the photo by adding more white color to it.

- Smoothens selected parts of the image, such as skin imperfections.

- Adjusts the sharpness of the picture. Increasing the sharpness will make the picture appear more detailed.

- Focuses on a specific area of a picture while making the rest of the picture out of focus.

- Converts the image into a grayscale picture, allowing you to add color to specific areas of the picture using a paintbrush.

5. Touch **Done** in the upper right-hand corner of the Picture Editing screen when you are finished. Your changes are saved.

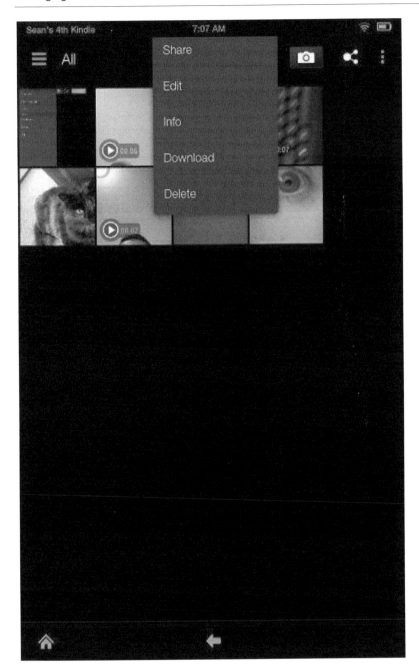

Figure 5: Picture Options

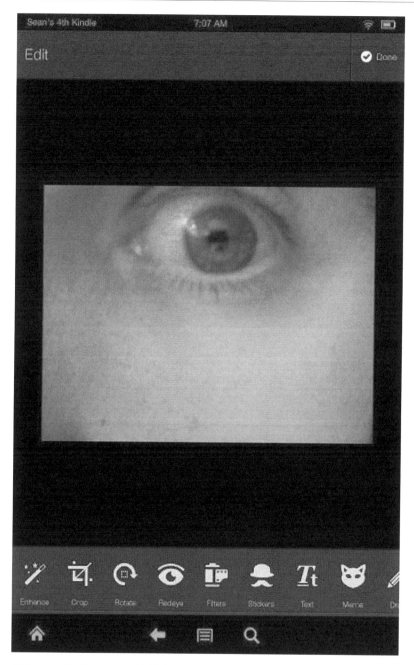

Figure 6: Picture Editing Screen

5. Cropping a Picture

You may crop a picture to use a specific piece of it. To crop a picture:

1. Touch **Photos** at the top of the library. The thumbnails of the pictures on your device appear.
2. Touch and hold the picture that you wish to edit. The Picture options appear.
3. Touch **Edit**. The Picture Editing screen appears.
4. Touch the icon at the bottom of the screen. Crop marks appear on the picture, as shown in **Figure** 7.
5. Touch one of the markers and drag it in any direction to change the size of the crop.
6. Touch anywhere inside of the crop and drag it in any direction to adjust the area that is cropped. You can also touch one of the ratios at the bottom of the screen to change the dimensions of the crop.
7. Touch **Apply** in the upper right-hand corner of the screen. The picture is cropped and the Editing screen appears.
8. Touch **Done** in the upper right-hand corner of the screen. Your crop is saved.

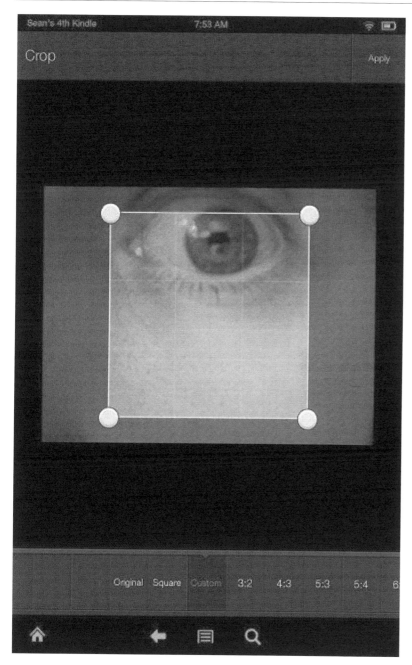

Figure 7: Crop Marks on a Picture

6. Flipping or Rotating a Picture

You may rotate a photo in 90 degree increments, flip it to view it upside down or as a mirror image, or rotate it by a few degrees at a time. To flip or rotate a picture:

1. Touch **Photos** at the top of the library. The thumbnails of the pictures on your device appear.
2. Touch and hold the picture that you wish to edit. The Picture options appear.
3. Touch **Edit**. The Picture Editing screen appears.
4. Touch the icon at the bottom of the screen. The Rotate screen appears, as shown in **Figure 8**.
5. Touch one of the following icons at the bottom of the screen to rotate or flip the picture accordingly:

- Rotates the picture 90 degrees to the left.

- Rotate the picture 90 degrees to the right.

- Flips the picture horizontally, creating a horizontal mirror image.

- Flips the picture vertically, creating a vertical mirror image.

6. You can also touch the slider and move it to the left or right to rotate the picture by up to 45 degrees in either direction.

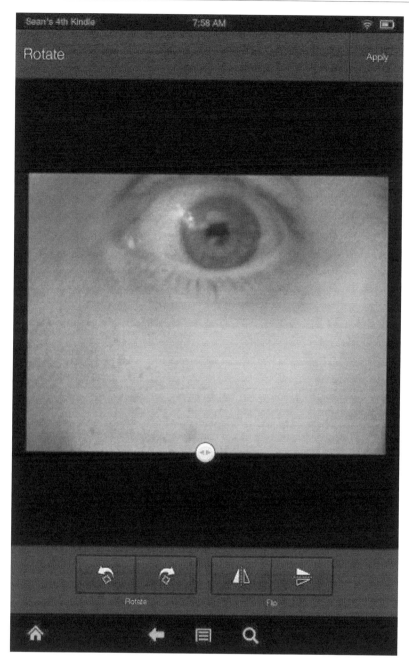

Figure 8: Rotate Screen

7. Deleting Pictures or Videos

Warning: Once a picture is deleted, there is no way to restore it.

To free up some space in the device's memory, try deleting some pictures. To delete pictures:

1. Touch **Photos** at the top of the library. The thumbnails of the pictures on your device appear.

2. Touch the ⬛ icon in the upper right-hand corner of the screen. 'Delete' appears.

3. Touch **Delete**. A 🗑 icon appears at the top of the screen.

4. Touch each picture or video that you wish to delete. A ☑ appears on each selected photo, as shown in **Figure 9**.

5. Touch the 🗑 icon at the top of the screen. A confirmation dialog appears.

6. Touch **OK**. The selected picture and videos are deleted.

Figure 9: Selected Photos

8. Importing and Exporting Pictures Using a PC or Mac

Pictures that you have taken or obtained elsewhere can be imported to the Kindle Fire HDX. Refer to *"Connecting the Kindle Fire HDX to a PC or Mac"* on page 23 to learn how to import or export pictures. Double-click the 'Pictures' folder in step 4 to access the folder where all pictures are stored on your device.

9. Sharing a Picture or Video via Email

You may share up to 10 pictures or one video by attaching the media to an email. To share a picture or video:

1. Touch **Photos** at the top of the library. The thumbnails of the pictures on your device appear

2. Touch the ![icon] icon in the upper right-hand corner of the screen. The ![icon] icon appears at the top of the screen, as shown in **Figure 10**.

3. Touch each picture that you would like to share. A ![icon] appears on each selected photo.

4. Touch the ![icon] icon. The Compose screen appears with the selected photos attached, as shown in **Figure 11**.

5. Enter the email address of the recipient and an optional subject. You can also enter optional text by touching the white space beneath the attached pictures.

6. Touch the ![icon] button in the upper right-hand corner of the screen. The email is sent with the attached pictures.

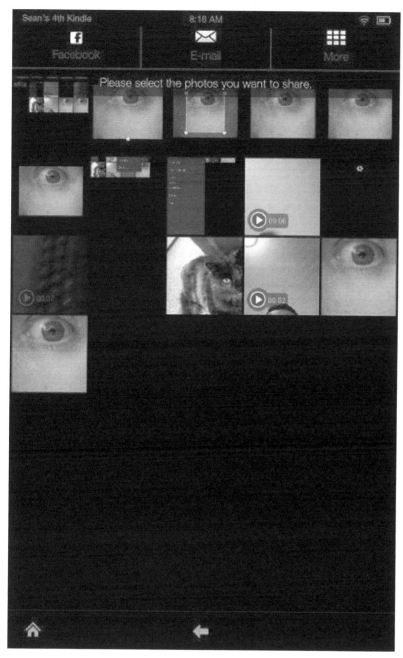

Figure 10: Email Envelope

Figure 11: Compose Screen with Attached Pictures

Making Video Calls Using Skype

Table of Contents

1. Registering for a Skype Account

Before you can use Skype to make a video call, you must first create a Skype account. To register for a Skype account, visit the **Skype Account Creation** web page at **https://login.skype.com/account/signup-form** on your computer or mobile device (computer is recommended to register more quickly). Enter all of the required profile information and click the I agree - Continue button. Your new Skype account is created and you may now sign in to Skype on the Kindle Fire HDX. Refer to *"Signing In to the Skype Application"* below to learn how.

2. Signing In to the Skype Application

Before you can place any calls using Skype, you must first download and sign in using your Skype account. Refer to *"Registering for a Skype Account"* above to learn how to create one. Refer to *"Buying an Application"* on page 189 to learn how to use the Amazon application store. To sign in to the Skype application:

1. Touch **Apps** at the top of the library. The App Library appears, as shown in **Figure 1**.

2. Touch the ⓢ icon. The Skype application opens and the Welcome screen appears, as shown in **Figure 2**.
3. Touch **Sign in with a Skype account**. The Sign In screen appears, as shown in **Figure 3**.
4. Enter your Skype name and password and touch **Sign in**. The Skype Home screen appears, as shown in **Figure 4**.

Figure 1: Apps Library

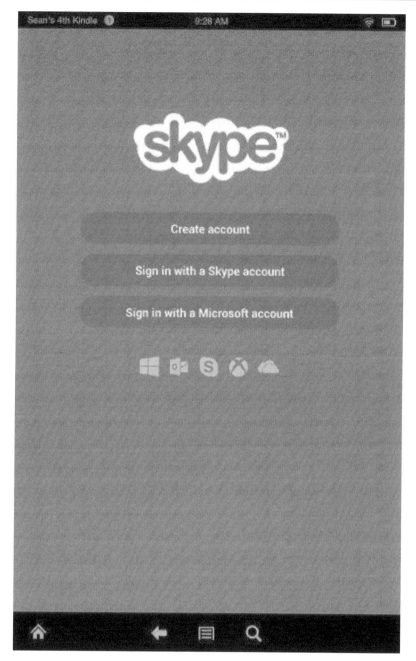

Figure 2: Skype Welcome Screen

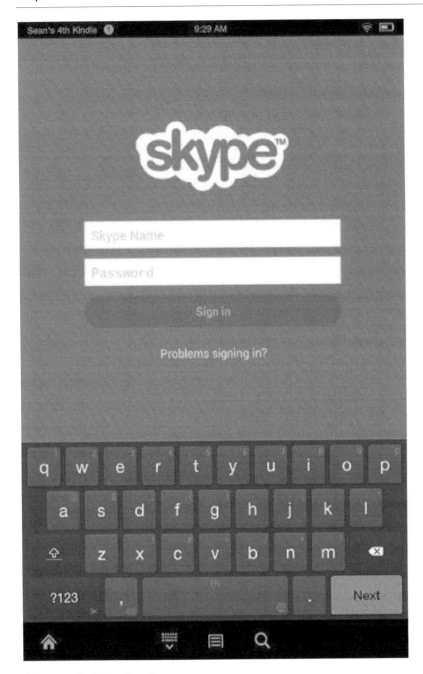

Figure 3: Sign In Screen

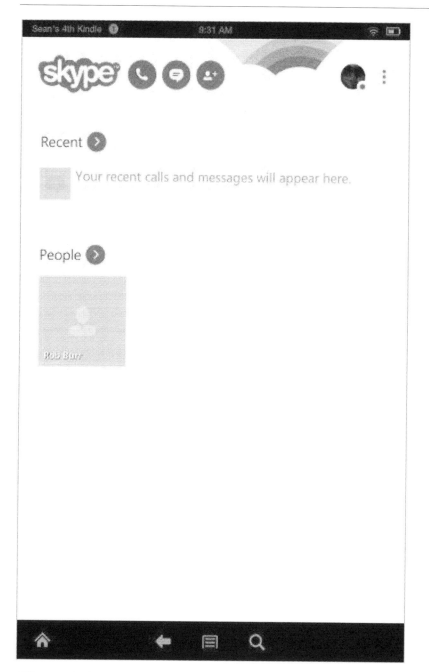

Figure 4: Skype Home Screen

3. Initiating a Skype Video Call

You can make video calls using the Skype application. To place a Skype video call:

1. Touch the name of a contact under 'People' on the Home screen. The chat history with the selected contact appears, as shown in **Figure 5**.

2. Touch the icon at the top of the screen. A video call is initiated. The video call is connected when the recipient accepts it, as shown in **Figure 6**.

3. Touch anywhere on the screen to bring up the call controls, as shown in **Figure 7**.

4. Touch the icon. The video call ends.

Figure 5: Chat History

Figure 6: Video Call Connected

Figure 7: Call Controls

4. Managing Skype Contacts

Skype contacts are stored in the Skype Address Book. You may add, edit, or remove contacts from within the Skype application.

To add a Skype contact:

1. Touch the ⊕ icon at the top of the Skype Home screen. The Add Contact menu appears, as shown in **Figure 8**.
2. Touch **Add People** or **Add Number**, depending on your preference.
3. If you touched **Add People**, enter the Skype name of the person. Matching results automatically appear as you type. Touch the name of the person and then touch **Add to contacts**. A request is sent to the person, and he or she must accept it.
4. If you touched **Add Number**, enter the name and number of the person and touch **Done**. The phone number is added to your contacts.

To edit a Skype contact:

1. Touch the name of the contact that you wish to edit under 'People'. The Chat History screen appears.
2. Touch the ⋮ icon in the upper right-hand corner of the screen. The Contact menu appears, as shown in **Figure 9**.
3. Touch **Edit contact**. The Contact Editing screen appears on the left-hand side of the screen, as shown in **Figure 10**. Touch **Add number** to add a phone number for the contact, if you wish.

To remove a Skype contact, touch the name of the contact under 'People' on the Skype Home screen, and then touch **Remove contact**. The contact is removed.

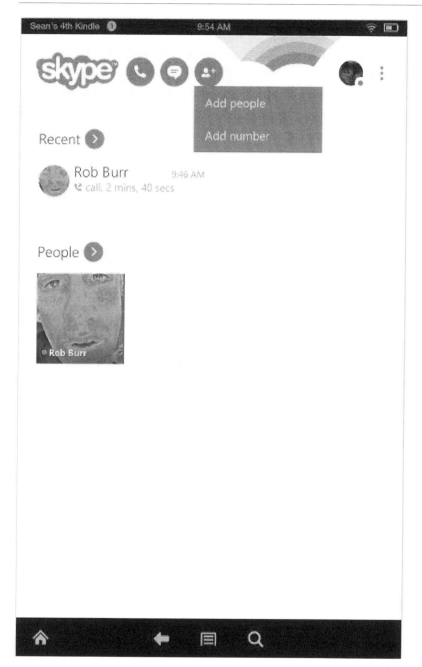

Figure 8: Add Contact Menu

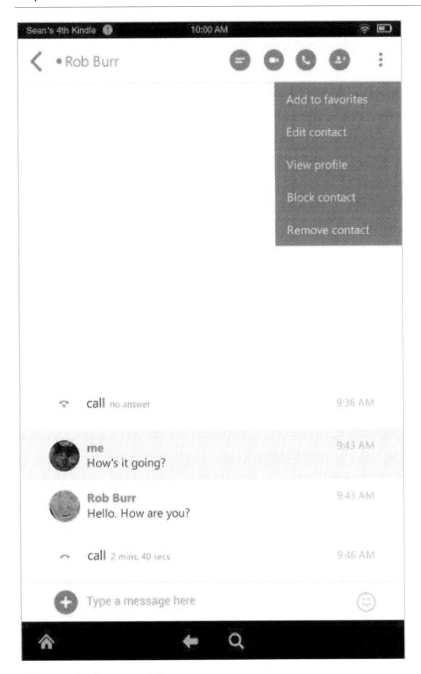

Figure 9: Contact Menu

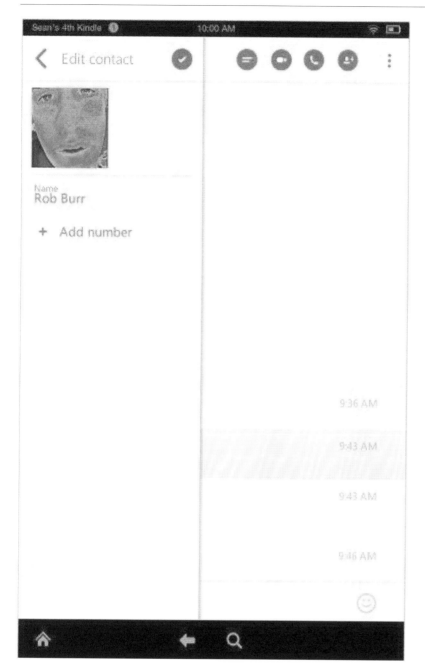

Figure 10: Contact Editing Screen

5. Signing Out of Skype

In order to avoid receiving unwanted Skype calls, you may wish to sign out of Skype. To sign out of Skype, touch your Skype Profile icon in the upper right-hand corner of the screen, as outlined in **Figure 11**. Your Profile menu appears, as shown in **Figure 12**. Touch **Sign out**. You are signed out of Skype.

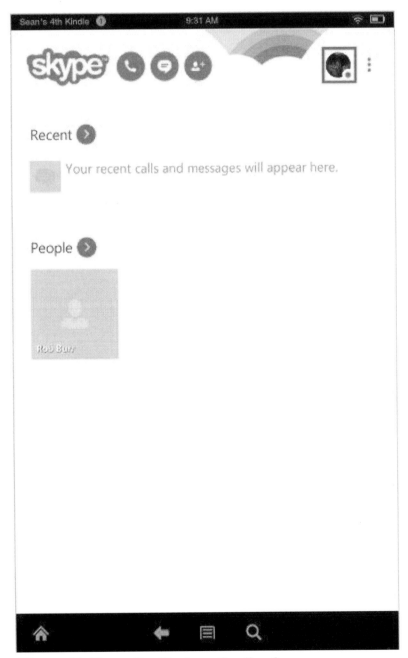

Figure 11: Skype Profile Icon Outlined

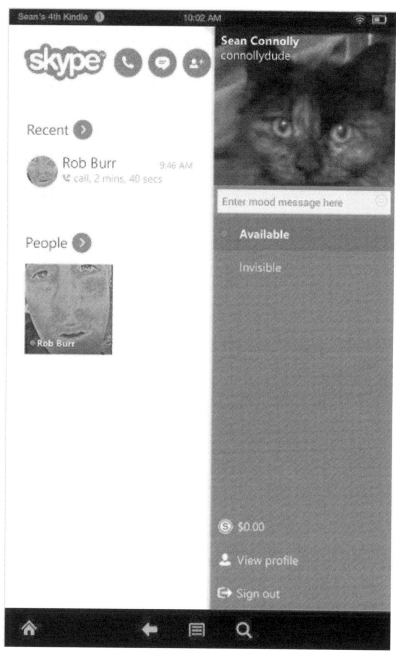

Figure 12: Profile Menu

Managing Contacts

Managing Contacts

Table of Contents

1. Adding a New Contact
2. Editing a Contact's Information
3. Deleting a Contact
4. Sharing a Contact's Information

---

1. Adding a New Contact

The Kindle Fire HDX allows you to manage your contacts using the Contacts application. To add a new contact:

1. Touch **Apps** at the top of the Library. The Apps Library appears, as shown in **Figure 1**.

2. Touch the icon. The Address Book opens, as shown in **Figure 2**.

3. Touch the button in the upper right-hand corner of the screen. The Synchronization menu appears, as shown in **Figure 3**. The appearance of this menu will vary based on the accounts that you have added to your device.

4. Touch the account with which you would like to sync the new contact. The contact will appear in any address book on all devices registered with the selected account. The New Contact screen appears, as shown in **Figure 4**.

5. Touch each field and enter the desired information. Touch the button in the upper right-hand corner of the screen. The contact is added to your address book.

Figure 1: Apps Library

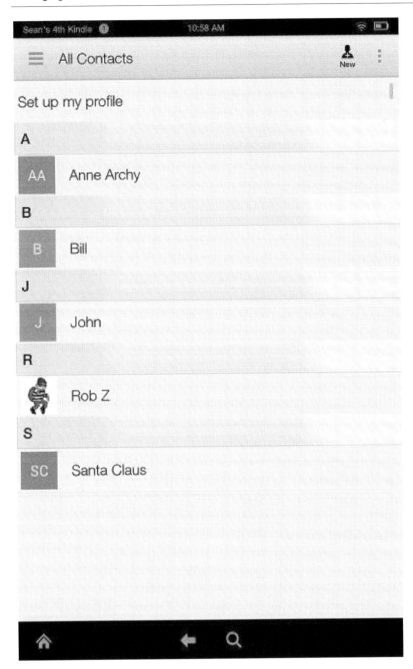

Figure 2: Address Book

Figure 3: Synchronization Menu

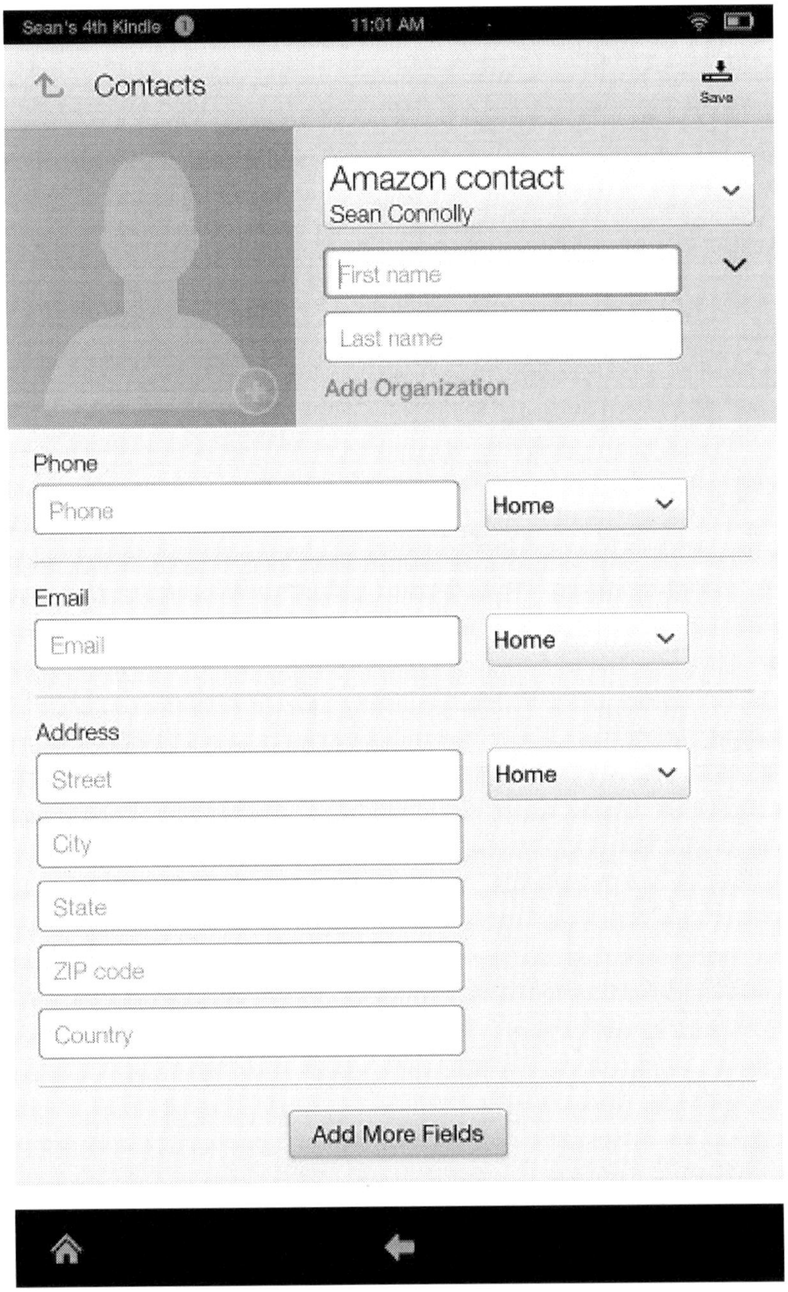

Figure 4: New Contact Screen

2. Editing a Contact's Information

Edit a contact's information to add additional data, such as an email address or additional phone number. To edit an existing contact's information:

1. Touch **Apps** at the top of the Library. The Apps screen appears.

2. Touch the ![icon] icon. The Address Book opens.
3. Touch and hold a contact's name. The Contact Info menu appears, as shown in **Figure 5**.
4. Touch **Edit**. The contact's information appears.
5. Touch each field to edit the contact's information. Touch the ![button] button in the upper right-hand corner of the screen. The contact's information is saved.

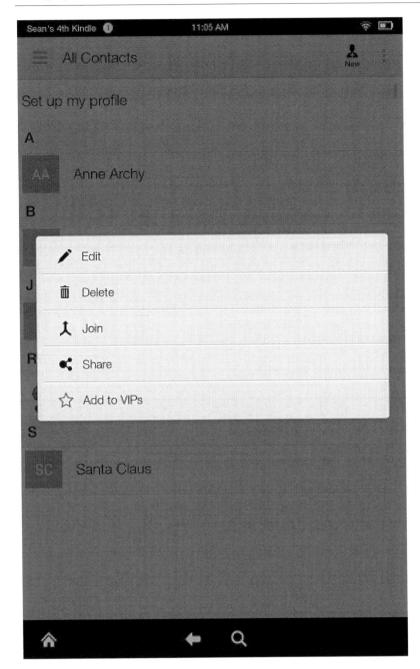

Figure 5: Contact Info Menu

3. Deleting a Contact

Free up memory by deleting contacts from the Kindle Fire HDX. To delete an unwanted contact:

1. Touch **Apps** at the top of the Library. The Apps screen appears.

2. Touch the icon. The Address Book application opens.
3. Touch and hold a contact's name. The Contact Info menu appears.
4. Touch **Delete**. A confirmation dialog appears.
5. Touch **OK**. The contact is deleted.

4. Sharing a Contact's Information

You can share a contact's information with others via email. To share a contact's information:

1. Touch **Apps** at the top of the Library. The Apps screen appears.

2. Touch the icon. The Address Book opens.
3. Touch and hold a contact's name. The Contact Info menu appears.
4. Touch **Share**. The New Email screen appears with the contact's information attached, as shown in **Figure 6**.
5. Enter the recipient's email address and an optional subject. You can also enter an optional message in the white space beneath the attached contact.

6. Touch the button in the upper right-hand corner of the screen. The contact's information is shared.

Figure 6: New Email Screen with Contact's Information Attached

Using the Silk Web Browser

Table of Contents

1. Navigating to a Web Page

The Kindle Fire HDX has a built-in Web browser called Silk. To navigate to a web page using its web address:

1. Touch **Web** at the top of the Library. The Silk browser opens, as shown in **Figure 1**. Touch the top of the library and slide your finger to the left if you do not see 'Web'.
2. Touch the address field at the top of the screen. The virtual keyboard appears.
3. Enter a web address and touch **Go**. The Silk browser navigates to the web page.

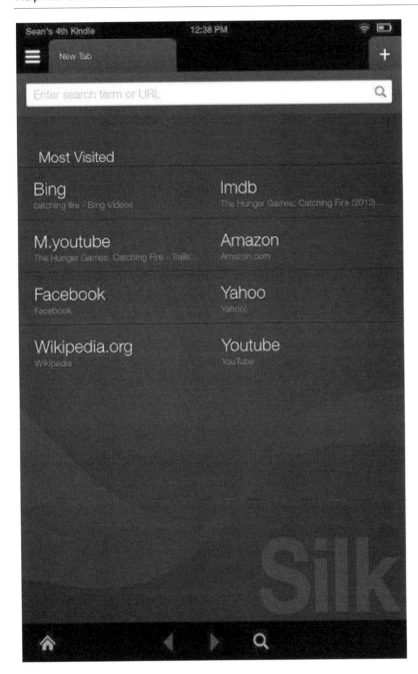

Figure 1: Silk Browser

2. Adding Bookmarks

Web pages can be stored as bookmarks for faster access. To add a web page to your bookmarks:

1. Navigate to a web page. Refer to *"Navigating to a Web Page"* on page 171 to learn how.
2. Touch the ▣ icon at the bottom of the screen. The Silk menu appears, as shown in **Figure 2**.
3. Touch **Add Bookmark**. The Add Bookmark dialog appears, as shown in **Figure 3**.
4. Touch the 'Name' field and enter a custom name for the bookmark, if desired. Touch **OK**. The web page is saved to bookmarks and appears as the last item in the last row.

Note: Touch the left edge of the screen while using the Silk browser, slide your finger to the right, and touch **Bookmarks** *to view a list of your bookmarks.*

Figure 2: Silk Menu

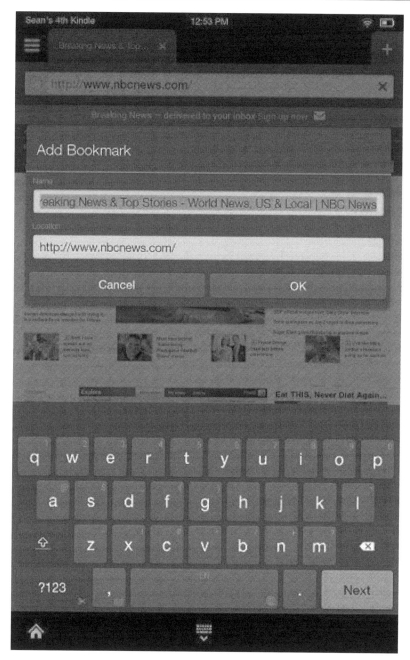

Figure 3: Add Bookmark Dialog

3. Managing Tabs

Up to ten tabs can be opened at once and displayed at the top of the Silk browser. Use the following tips to manage tabs:

- Touch the ![+] icon in the upper right-hand corner of the Silk browser to open a new tab.
- Touch the ![X] icon on a tab to close it.
- Touch a tab and drag your finger to the left or right to view more open tabs when more than three tabs are open.

Note: Refer to "Tips and Tricks" on page 248 to learn how to close all tabs at once.

4. Using Links

In addition to touching a link to navigate to its destination, there are other link options. Touch and hold a link to see all of the link options, as follows:

- **Open in new tab** - Opens the link in a new tab without closing the existing one.
- **Open in Background Tab** - Opens the link in a new tab without switching to it. The current tab remains open.
- **Bookmark Link** - Adds the link to the bookmarks.
- **Share Link** - Copies the link into an email or a friend's Facebook wall, depending on your selection.
- **Copy link URL** - Copies the link to the clipboard, allowing it to be pasted in any text field.
- **Save Link** - Saves the current web page to your device where it can be viewed even if you are not connected to the internet. You will not be able to access any links on the web page when viewing it offline. Touch the left edge of the screen, slide your finger to the right, and touch **Downloads** to view a list of downloaded web pages.

5. Searching a Web Page for a Word or Phrase

While surfing the web, any web page can be searched for a word or phrase. To search a web page:

1. Touch the ![menu] button at the bottom of the screen. The Silk menu appears.
2. Touch **Find in Page**. The Search field and virtual keyboard appear.

3. Enter a search word or phrase. The search results are highlighted as you type, as shown in **Figure 4**. Touch the ▲ and ▼ buttons to the left of the search field to scroll through the results on the web page.

Figure 4: Matching Results Highlighted

6. Viewing Recently Visited Websites

The Kindle Fire HDX stores all recently visited websites in its Browsing History. To view the History, touch the left edge of the screen and slide your finger to the right. The Silk options appear, as shown in **Figure 5**. Touch **History**. The Browsing History screen appears, as shown in **Figure 6**.

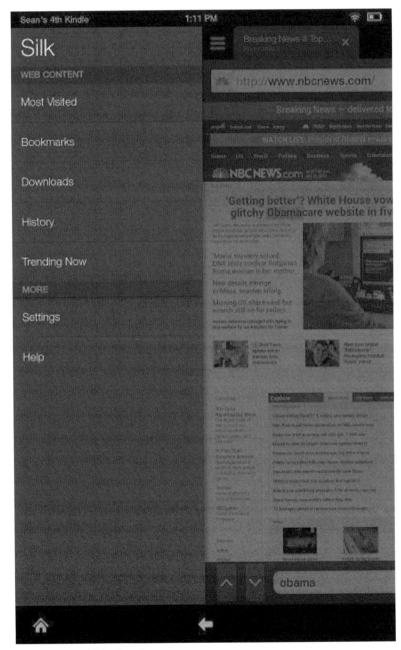

Figure 5: Silk Options

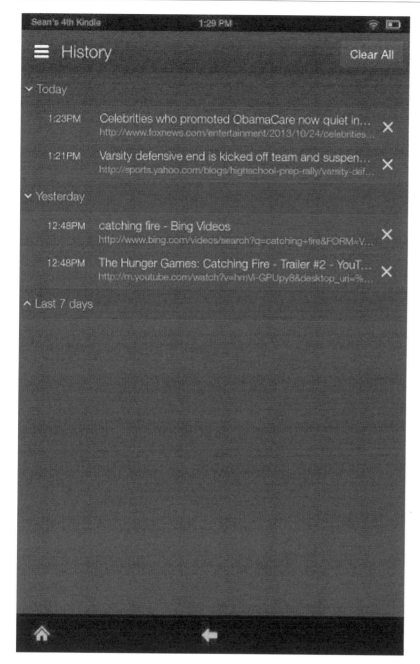

Figure 6: Browsing History

7. Blocking Pop-Up Windows

Some websites may have pop-up windows that will interfere with web browsing. To block pop-ups:

1. Touch the left edge of the screen and slide your finger to the right. The Silk options appear.
2. Touch **Settings**. The Browser Settings screen appears, as shown in **Figure 7**.
3. Touch **Block pop-up windows**. The Block Pop-Up Windows menu appears.
4. Touch **Always**. Pop-up windows will now be blocked.

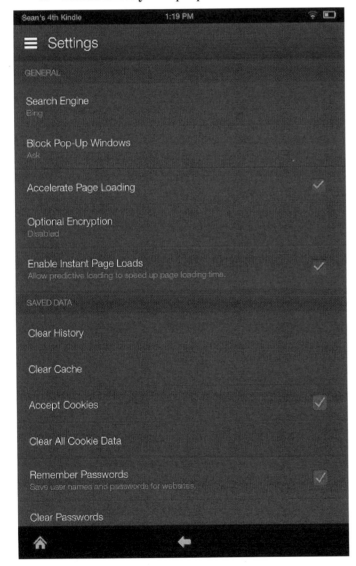

Figure 7: Browser Settings Screen

8. Changing the Default Search Engine

When you enter a search term in the web address field, the default search engine is used to perform the search. The default search engine is Google. To change the default search engine:

1. Touch the left edge of the screen and slide your finger to the right. The Silk options appear.
2. Touch **Settings**. The Browser Settings screen appears.
3. Touch **Search engine**. A list of available search engines appears, as shown in **Figure 8**.
4. Touch your preferred search engine. The new default search engine is set and will be used for all searches.

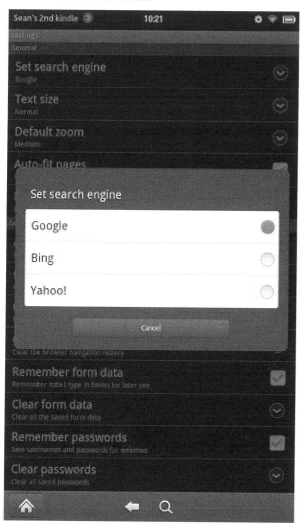

Figure 8: List of Available Search Engines

9. Saving Passwords in Forms

The Silk browser can automatically save the passwords that you enter in forms. To save passwords in forms:

1. Touch the left edge of the screen and slide your finger to the right. The Silk options appear.
2. Touch **Settings**. The Browser Settings screen appears.
3. Touch **Remember passwords**. The ☑ appears to the right of 'Remember passwords' and the feature is turned on.
4. Touch **Remember passwords** again. The ☑ disappears and the feature is turned off.

Managing Applications

1. Searching for an Application in the Amazon App Store

There are two ways to search for applications in the App Store on the Kindle Fire HDX:

Manual Search

To search for an application manually:

1. Touch **Apps** at the top of the library. The Apps Library appears, as shown in **Figure 1**.
2. Touch **Store** in the upper right-hand corner of the screen. The Apps Store opens, as shown in **Figure 2**.
3. Touch the 🔍 icon at the top of the screen. The virtual keyboard appears.
4. Enter the name of an application and touch the 🔍 key. All matching applications appear, as shown in **Figure 3**.

Browse by Category

To browse applications by category:
1. Touch **Apps** at the top of the library. The Apps Library appears.
2. Touch **Store** in the upper right-hand corner of the screen. The Apps Store opens.
3. Touch the left edge of the screen and slide your finger to the right. The App Store menu appears, as shown in **Figure 4**.
4. Touch **Browse Categories**. A list of categories appears, as shown in **Figure 5**.

5. Touch a category, such as **Games**, **Entertainment**, or **Music**. All of the applications available for that category appear.

Figure 1: Apps Library

Figure 2: Apps Store

Figure 3: Matching Applications

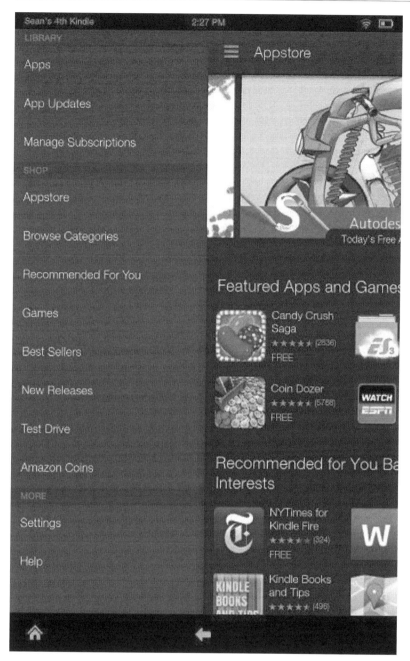

Figure 4: App Store Menu

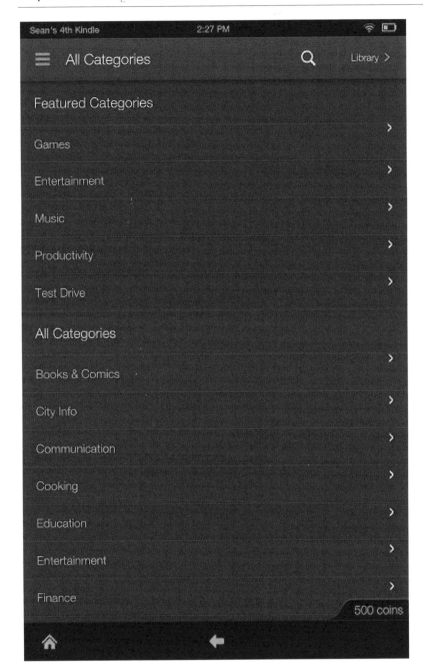

Figure 5: List of Categories

2. Buying an Application

Applications can be purchased directly from the Kindle Fire HDX using the Amazon App Store. To buy an application:

Warning: Before purchasing an application, make sure that you want it. There are no refunds for applications in the Amazon App Store.

1. Find the application that you wish to purchase. Refer to *"Searching for an Application in the Amazon App Store"* on page 183 to learn how.
2. Touch the name of the application. The Application description appears, as shown in **Figure 6**.

3. Touch the price of the application or touch the **FREE** button.

   The **Get App** button appears.

4. Touch the **Get App** button. The application is purchased and downloaded to your Apps library.

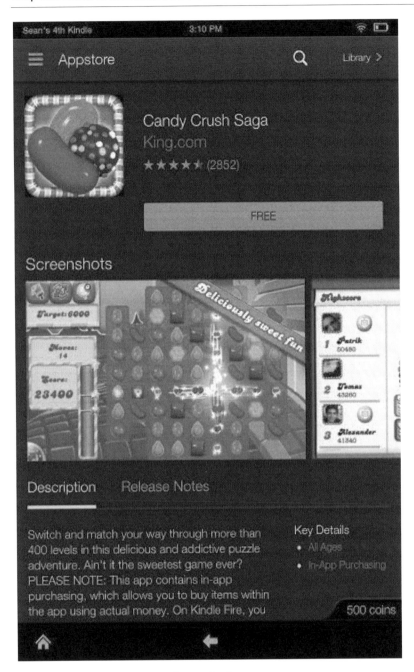

Figure 6: Application Description

3. Archiving an Application

In order to free up memory on the device, you can remove applications from the Kindle Fire HDX and store them in the Amazon cloud. Any application that is removed can always be downloaded later using a Wi-Fi connection. To remove an application:

1. Touch **Apps** at the top of the library. The Apps Library appears.
2. Touch and hold an application icon. The Application options appear above the icon, as shown in **Figure 7**.
3. Touch **Remove from Device**. A confirmation dialog appears.
4. Touch **OK**. The application is removed from the Kindle Fire HDX.

Figure 7: Application Options

4. Managing Applications on the Home Screen

Any application can be added to the Home screen for easy access. You can view the Home screen by touching the Library and moving your finger up.

To add an application to the Home screen:

1. Touch **Apps** at the top of the library. The Apps Library appears.
2. Touch and hold an application icon. The Application options appear above the icon.
3. Touch **Add to Home**. The application is added to the Home screen.

To remove applications from the Home screen:

1. Touch and hold an application on the Home screen. 'Remove' appears in the upper left-hand corner of the screen.
2. Remove your finger from the screen. An orange box appears around the application that you selected.
3. Touch each application that you wish to remove from the Home screen. An orange box appears around each selected application, as shown in **Figure 8**.
4. Touch **Remove**. The selected applications are removed from the Home screen.

To move an application around on the Home screen, touch and hold it and drag it to the desired location.

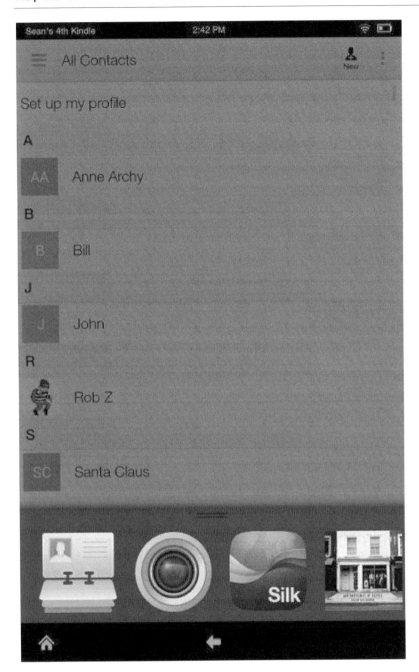

Figure 8: Selected Applications

5. Switching to Another Application while Using an App

While using an application, you can view a list of the currently open applications, and switch to one. To switch to another application, touch the bottom edge of the screen. A list of open applications appears, as shown in **Figure 9**. Touch an application in the list. The application is opened. You can also touch the list and slide your finger to the left or right to view more open applications.

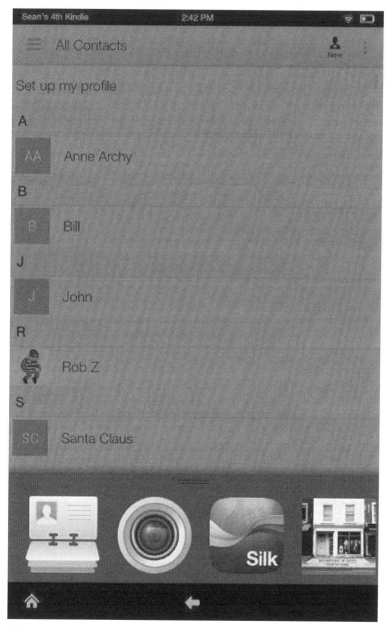

Figure 9: List of Open Applications

6. Reporting an Issue with an Application

If an application malfunctions or is offensive in any way, you can report the issue to Amazon, who will get in touch with the developer to address your concern. To report an issue with an application:

1. Touch **Apps** at the top of the library. The Apps Library appears.
2. Touch **Store** in the upper right-hand corner of the screen. The Apps Store opens.
3. Find the application that you wish to report. Refer to *"Searching for an Application in the Amazon App Store"* on page 183 to learn how.
4. Touch the title of the application. The Application description appears.
5. Touch the screen and move your finger up to scroll down to the bottom of the description. Touch **Report an Issue**. The Issue Type menu appears, as shown in **Figure 10**.
6. Touch the type of issue you are having. The appropriate reporting screen appears. Follow the instructions on the screen, which vary depending on your issue.

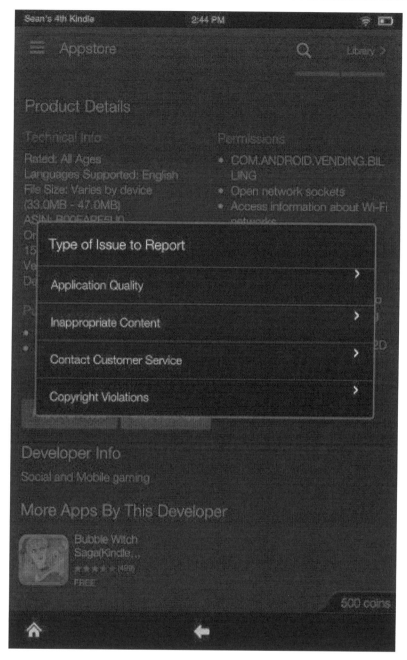

Figure 10: Issue Type Menu

7. Test Driving an Application

The Amazon application store allows you to test an application for ten minutes before downloading it. To test drive an application:

1. Touch **Apps** at the top of the library. The Apps Library appears.
2. Touch the left edge of the screen and slide your finger to the right. The Application Library menu appears, as shown in **Figure 11**.
3. Touch **Test Drive**. A list of applications that are available for Test Drive appears, as shown in **Figure 12**.
4. Touch an application in the list. The application description appears.
5. Touch **Test Drive**. The application opens in Test Drive, as shown in **Figure 13**.
   Touch **Quit** in the upper left-hand corner of the screen at any time to close Test Drive.

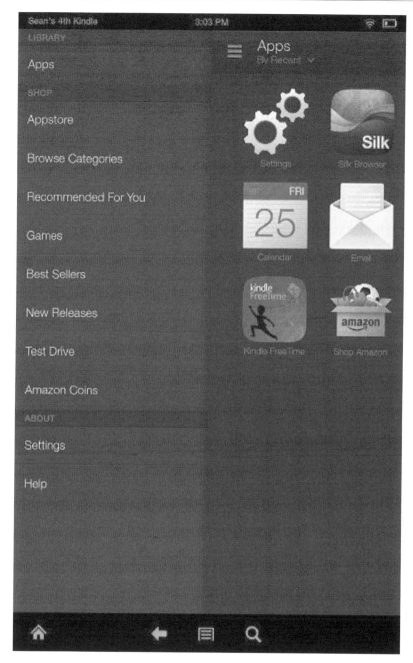

Figure 11: Application Library Menu

Figure 12: List of Applications Available for Test Drive

Figure 13: Application in Test Drive

Adjusting the Settings

Table of Contents

1. Adjusting the Brightness

The brightness of the screen can be changed. You can also have the device set the brightness automatically, depending on the current lighting conditions. To adjust the brightness:

1. Touch the time at the top of the screen and slide your finger down. The Quick Settings Banner appears, as shown in **Figure 1**.

2. Touch the ☀ icon. The Brightness bar appears. Automatic Brightness is enabled by default.

3. Touch the On Off switch next to 'Auto-Brightness'. Automatic Brightness is turned off and the brightness bar appears.

4. Touch the ○ on the ══○══ bar and drag it to the left to decrease the brightness or to the right to increase it. The brightness is adjusted accordingly.

Figure 1: Quick Settings Banner

2. Setting Up Parental Controls

You can set up parental controls to restrict the ways in which your children use the Kindle Fire HDX. To set up parental controls:

1. Touch the time at the top of the screen and slide your finger down. The Quick Settings Banner appears.

2. Touch the ⚙ icon. The Settings screen appears, as shown in **Figure 2**.

3. Touch **Parental Controls**. The Parental Controls Settings screen appears, as shown in **Figure 3**.

4. Touch the [On | Off] switch next to 'Parental Controls'. Parental Controls are turned on and the Parental Controls Password screen appears, as shown in **Figure 4**.

5. Enter your preferred password twice and touch **Finish**. The Parental Controls password is set and a list of restriction options appears, as shown in **Figure 5**.

6. Touch **Unblocked** next to a feature to restrict it, or touch **Blocked** to allow it. Alternatively, touch the [On | Off] switch next to a feature to disable it, or touch the [On | Off] to enable it.

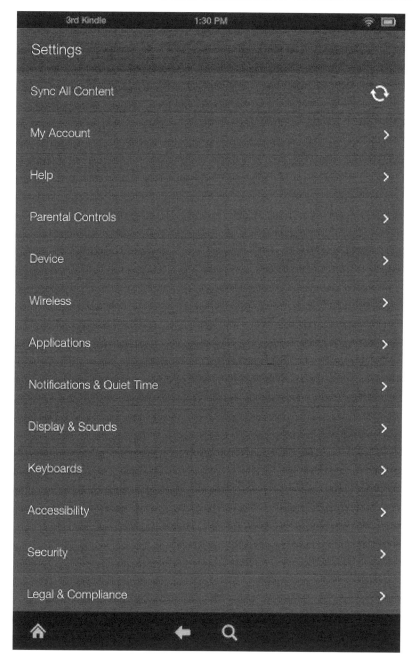

Figure 2: Settings Screen

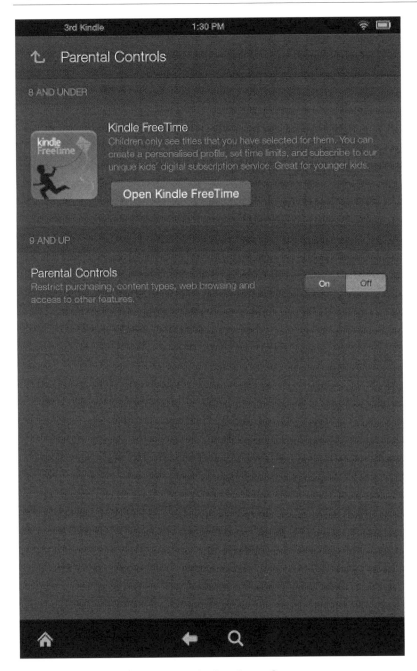

Figure 3: Parental Controls Settings Screen

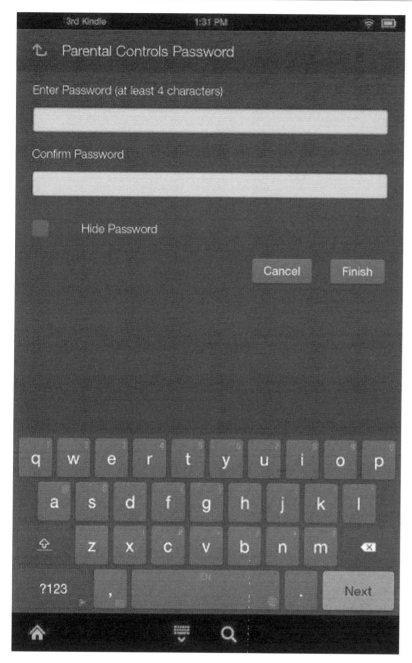

Figure 4: Parental Controls Password Screen

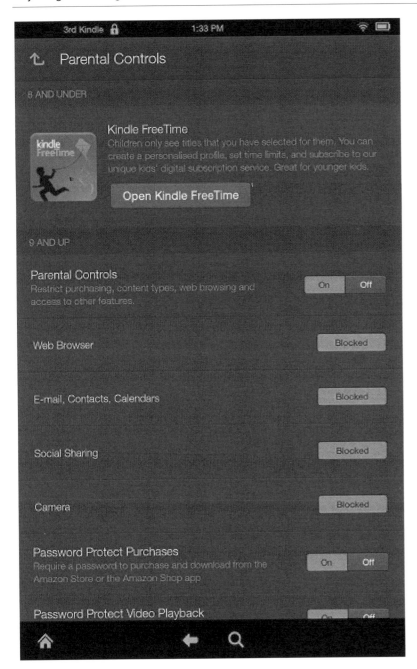

Figure 5: List of Restriction Options

3. Setting the System Language

The language that is used to display menus and options on the Kindle Fire HDX can be changed. To set the system language:

1. Touch the time at the top of the screen and slide your finger down. The Quick Settings Banner appears.
2. Touch the icon. The Settings screen appears.
3. Touch **Device**. The Device Settings screen appears, as shown in **Figure 6**.
4. Touch **Language**. A list of available languages appears, as shown in **Figure 7**.
5. Touch a language in the list. The selected language is applied to all menus and options.

Note: Any web content or downloaded media will not be translated to the system language.

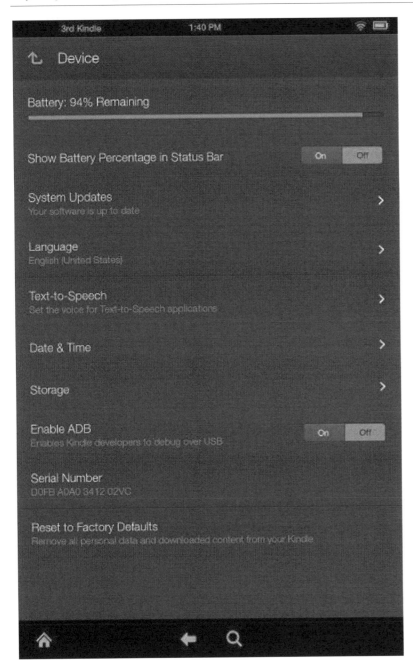

Figure 6: Device Settings Screen

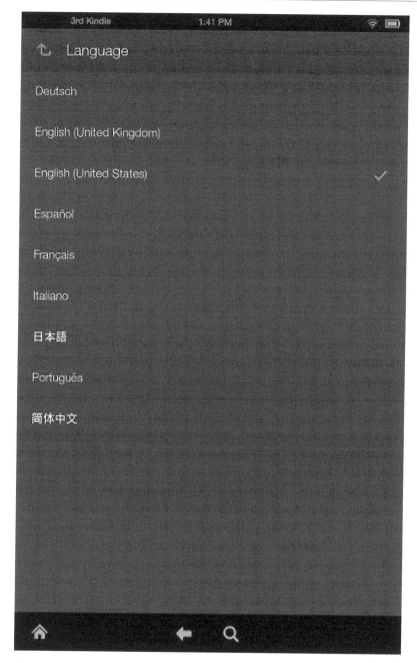

Figure 7: List of Available Languages

4. Setting the Text-to-Speech Language

The device allows you to select the voice and language that is used when using applications that support text-to-speech. To set the text-to-speech language:

1. Touch the time at the top of the screen and slide your finger down. The Quick Settings Banner appears.
2. Touch the ⚙ icon. The Settings screen appears.
3. Touch **Device**. The Device Settings screen appears.
4. Touch **Text-to-Speech**. The Text-to-Speech Settings screen appears, as shown in **Figure 8**. By default, there is only one voice installed on your device.
5. Touch **Download Additional Voices**. A list of downloadable voices appears, as shown in **Figure 9**.
6. Touch the language that you would like to download. The selected language is downloaded. When the download is finished, the language will appear in the Default Voice list, which is accessible from the Text-to-Speech Settings screen.

Note: Downloaded media will not be translated to the system language.

Figure 8: Text-to-Speech Settings Screen

Figure 9: List of Downloadable Voices

5. Setting the Time Zone

The Kindle Fire HDX will automatically set the time according to the time zone, even when you are traveling. To set the time zone:

1. Touch the time at the top of the screen and slide your finger down. The Quick Settings Banner appears.
2. Touch the icon. The Settings screen appears.
3. Touch **Device**. The Device Settings screen appears.
4. Touch **Date & Time**. The Date & Time Settings screen appears, as shown in **Figure 10**.
5. Touch **Select Time Zone**. A list of time zones appears, as shown in **Figure 11**.
6. Touch your current time zone. The time zone is set and the time will be automatically adjusted. Remember to change the time zone if you travel outside of the current one.

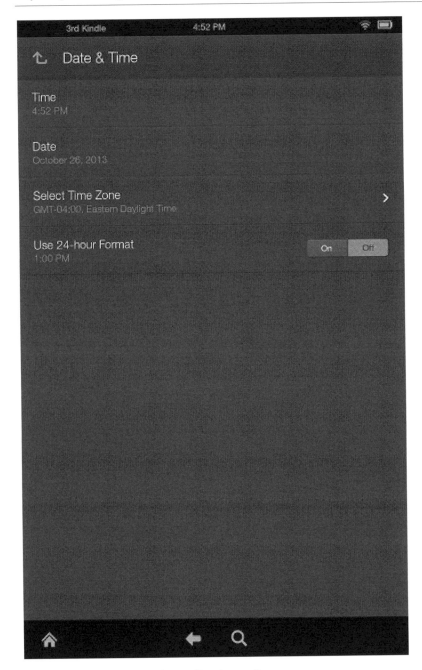

Figure 10: Date & Time Settings Screen

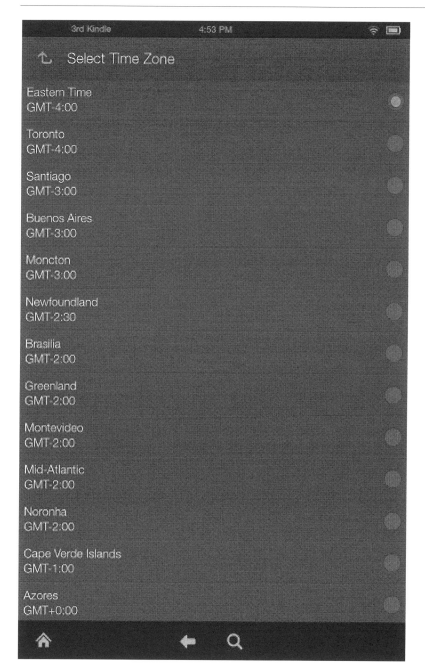

Figure 11: List of Time Zones

6. Turning Airplane Mode On or Off

Airplane Mode is used to turn off all wireless communications and, in certain instances, it is easier to turn it on rather than turn off the device entirely. To turn Airplane Mode on or off:

1. Touch the time at the top of the screen and slide your finger down. The Quick Settings Banner appears.

2. Touch the ⚙ icon. The Settings screen appears.

3. Touch **Wireless**. The Wireless Settings screen appears, as shown in **Figure 12**.

4. Touch the On Off switch next to Airplane Mode. The On Off switch appears and Airplane Mode is turned on.

5. Touch the On Off switch next to Airplane Mode. The On Off switch appears and Airplane Mode is turned off.

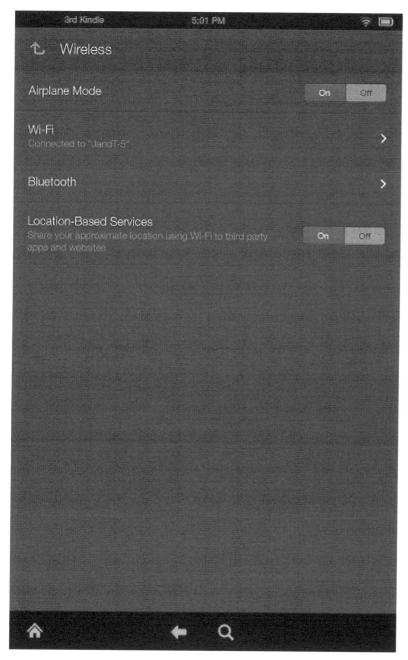

Figure 12: Wireless Settings Screen

7. Setting Up Wi-Fi

Connect to a Wi-Fi network to access the internet, which is required to stream and download media, surf the web, and use certain applications. To set up Wi-Fi:

1. Touch the time at the top of the screen and slide your finger down. The Quick Settings Banner appears.
2. Touch the ⚙ icon. The Settings screen appears.
3. Touch **Wireless**. The Wireless Settings screen appears.
4. Touch **Wi-Fi**. The Wi-Fi Settings screen appears.
5. Touch the [On Off] switch next to Wi-Fi. A list of Wi-Fi networks that are in range of your device appears, as shown in **Figure 13**.
6. Touch the network to which you would like to connect. The Network Password prompt appears, as shown in **Figure 14**. If you do not have a password protected network, the device immediately connects to the selected network.
7. Enter your network password (usually found on your wireless router), and touch **Connect**. The device connects to the selected Wi-Fi network.

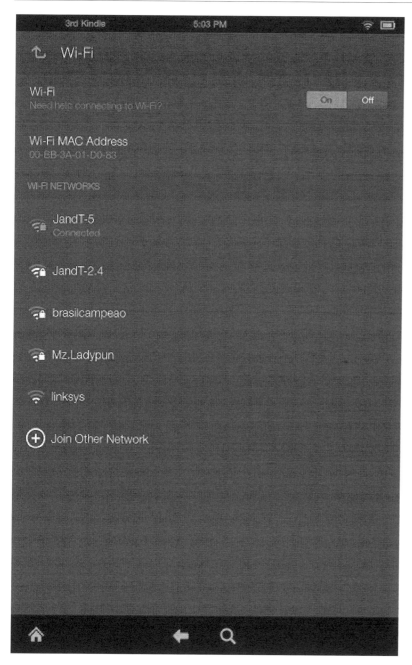

Figure 13: List of Wi-Fi Networks

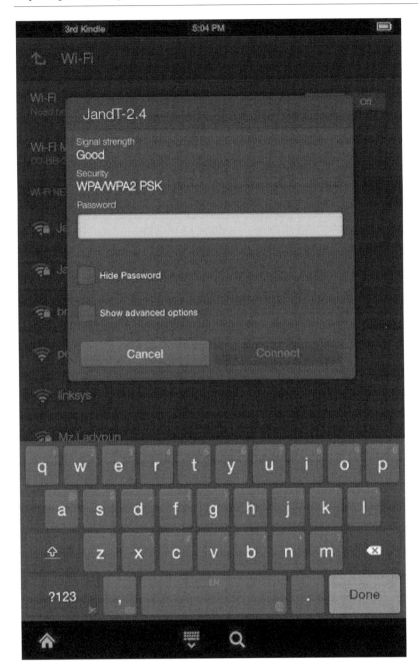

Figure 14: Network Password Prompt

8. Setting Up Bluetooth

Bluetooth allows you to connect to other devices to transfer media, or to wireless control devices, such as a keyboard. To set up Bluetooth:

1. Touch the time at the top of the screen and slide your finger down. The Quick Settings Banner appears.
2. Touch the ⚙ icon. The Settings screen appears.
3. Touch **Wireless**. The Wireless Settings screen appears.
4. Touch **Bluetooth**. The Bluetooth Settings screen appears.
5. Touch the [On Off] switch next to 'Bluetooth'. Bluetooth is turned on.
6. Touch **Pair a Bluetooth Device**. A list of discoverable devices appears, as shown in **Figure 15**. Make sure that Bluetooth is turned on your secondary device or keyboard.
7. Touch the name of a device in the list. The Kindle Fire HDX pairs with the selected device. You may need to enter a code on the secondary device before it can be paired.

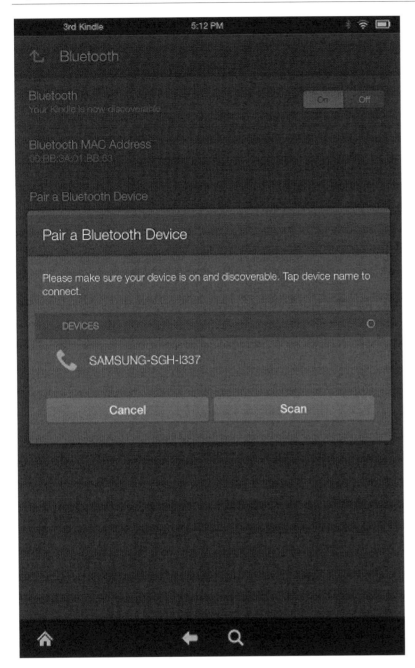

Figure 15: List of Discoverable Devices

9. Turning Location Services On or Off

Certain applications, such as navigation apps, need to determine your location. However, leaving Location Services turned on may drain your battery slightly more quickly. To turn Location Services on or off:

1. Touch the time at the top of the screen and slide your finger down. The Quick Settings Banner appears.
2. Touch the ⚙ icon. The Settings screen appears.
3. Touch **Wireless**. The Wireless Settings screen appears.
4. Touch the [On Off] switch next to 'Location-Based Services'. The [On Off] switch appears and Location Services are turned on.
5. Touch the [On Off] switch next to 'Location-Based Services'. The [On Off] switch appears and Location Services are turned off.

10. Managing Application Settings

Many applications, such the Amazon App Store, have customizable settings. For instance, you may turn Automatic Application Updates on or off for the Amazon App Store. To manage application settings:

1. Touch the time at the top of the screen and slide your finger down. The Quick Settings Banner appears.
2. Touch the ⚙ icon. The Settings screen appears.
3. Touch **Applications**. The Application Settings screen appears, as shown in **Figure 16**. Touch an application to edit its settings.

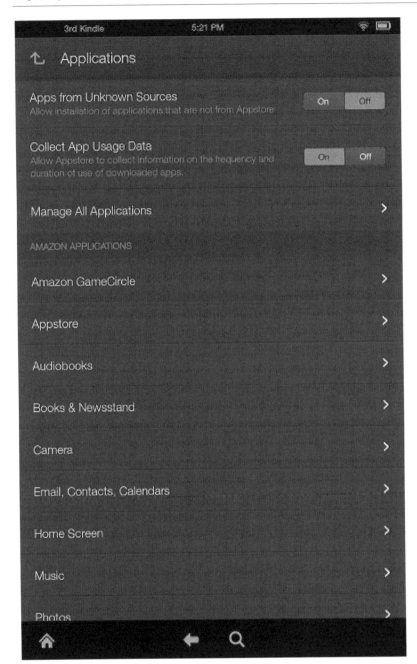

Figure 16: Application Settings Screen

11. Setting Up Quiet Time

The Quiet Time feature allows you to disable notifications while you are performing specific activities or during certain times of day. To set up Quiet Time:

1. Touch the time at the top of the screen and slide your finger down. The Quick Settings Banner appears.
2. Touch the [icon] icon. The Settings screen appears.
3. Touch **Notifications & Quiet Time**. The Notifications & Quiet Time screen appears, as shown in **Figure 17**.
4. Touch **Quiet Time**. The Quiet Time Settings screen appears, as shown in **Figure 18**.
5. Touch the [On Off] switch next to Scheduled Quiet Time. Scheduled Quiet Time is turned on, and a list of scheduling options appears, as shown in **Figure 19**.
6. Touch an option under 'TURN ON QUIET TIME WHENEVER I AM:'. A [✓] mark appears next to the selected option, and you will not be bothered by notifications while you are performing the selected actions.
7. Touch the [On Off] switch next to 'Schedule'. The Quiet Time Schedule window appears, as shown in **Figure 20**.
8. Set the times for which you would like to turn off notifications, and touch **Schedule Time**. Notifications are turned off for the selected time period.

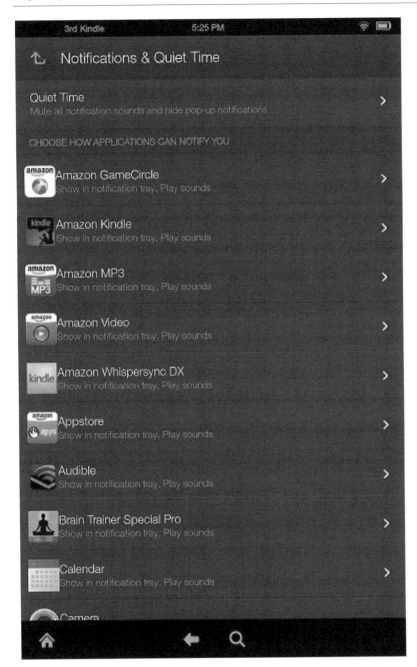

Figure 17: Notifications & Quiet Time Screen

Figure 18: Quiet Time Settings Screen

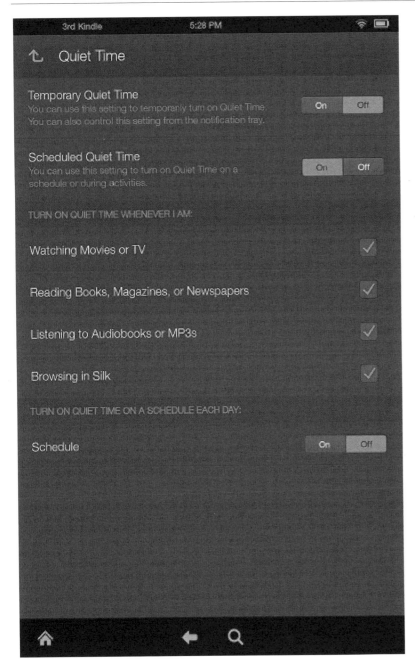

Figure 19: List of Scheduling Options

Figure 20: Quiet Time Schedule Window

12. Setting the Notification Sound

Whenever an application sends you a notification, the Kindle Fire HDX can play a sound. To set the notification sound:

1. Touch the time at the top of the screen and slide your finger down. The Quick Settings Banner appears.
2. Touch the icon. The Settings screen appears.
3. Touch **Display & Sounds**. The Display & Sounds Settings screen appears, as shown in **Figure 21**.
4. Touch **Notification Sound**. A list of available notification sounds appears, as shown in **Figure 22**.
5. Touch an option in the list. The selected notification sound is set.

Figure 21: Display & Sounds Settings Screen

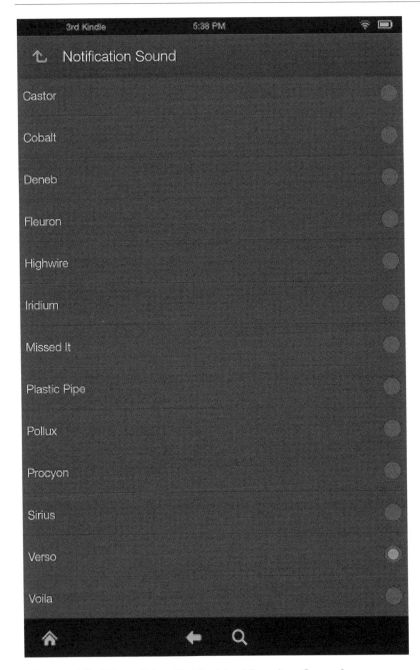

Figure 22: List of Available Notification Sounds

13. Setting the Screen Timeout

The display on your device can automatically turn off after a preset amount of time in order to preserve battery life. To set the screen timeout:

1. Touch the time at the top of the screen and slide your finger down. The Quick Settings Banner appears.
2. Touch the icon. The Settings screen appears.
3. Touch **Display & Sounds**. The Display & Sounds Settings screen appears.
4. Touch **Display Sleep**. A list of screen timeout options appears, as shown in **Figure 23**.
5. Touch an option in the list. The screen timeout is set.

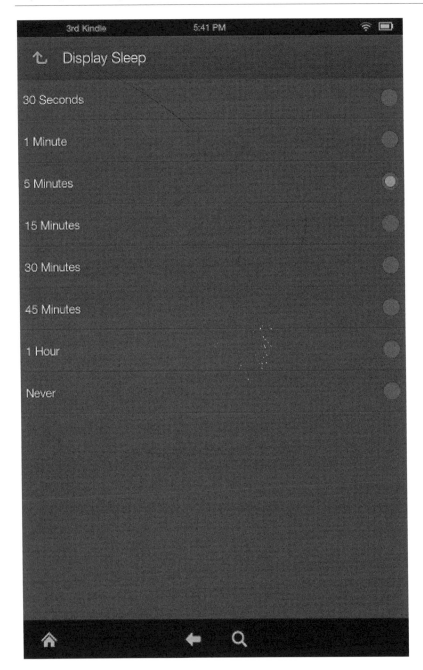

Figure 23: List of Screen Timeout Options

14. Adding International Keyboards

The Kindle Fire HDX allows you to input text using various international keyboards. To switch to another language while typing, touch and hold the space bar. To add an international keyboard:

1. Touch the time at the top of the screen and slide your finger down. The Quick Settings Banner appears.

2. Touch the ⚙ icon. The Settings screen appears.

3. Touch **Keyboards**. The Keyboards screen appears, as shown in **Figure 24**.

4. Touch **Languages**. A list of available international keyboards appears, as shown in **Figure 25**.

5. Touch a language in the list. A ☑ mark appears next to the language and the keyboard is added. You can also touch **Download Languages** if you do not see your preferred language in the list.

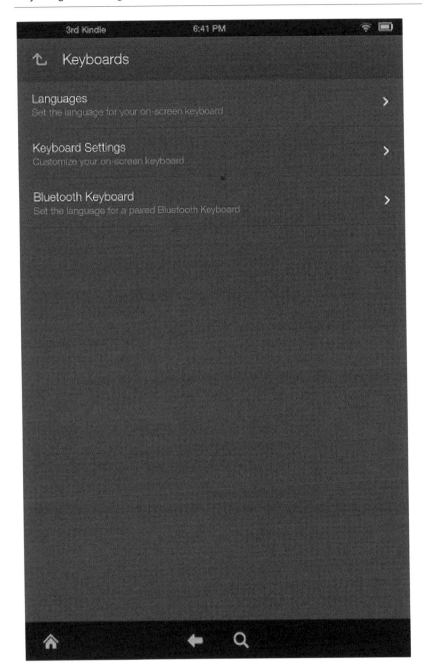

Figure 24: Keyboards Screen

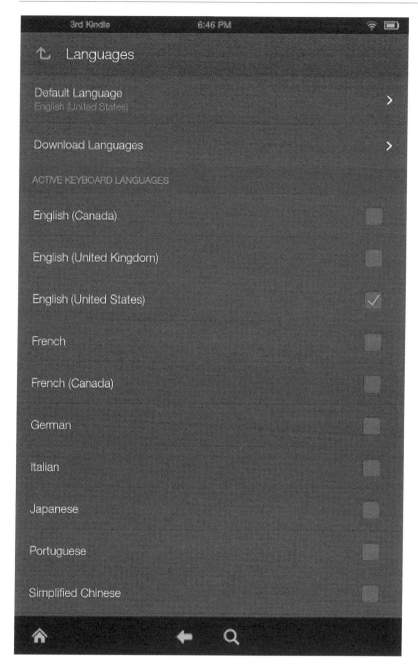

Figure 25: List of Available International Keyboards

15. Adjusting Keyboard Settings

The keyboard on the Kindle Fire HDX is highly customizable. To adjust keyboard settings:

- Touch the time at the top of the screen and slide your finger down. The Quick Settings Banner appears.
- Touch the ⚙ icon. The Settings screen appears.
- Touch **Keyboards**. The Keyboards screen appears.
- Touch **Keyboard Settings**. The Keyboard Settings screen appears, as shown in **Figure 26**.
- Touch one of the following features to turn it on or off:

  - **Sound on key press** - Turns keystroke sounds on or off.
  - **Auto-correction** - Corrects misspelled words as you type.
  - **Auto-capitalization** - Capitalizes words, such as those at the beginning of sentences or proper nouns, such as names.
  - **Next word prediction** - Studies your typing habits and suggests the next word in a sentence based on sentences that you have entered in the past.
  - **Check Spelling** - Underlines misspelled words.

Note: The On Off *switch next to a feature indicates that it is turned on.*

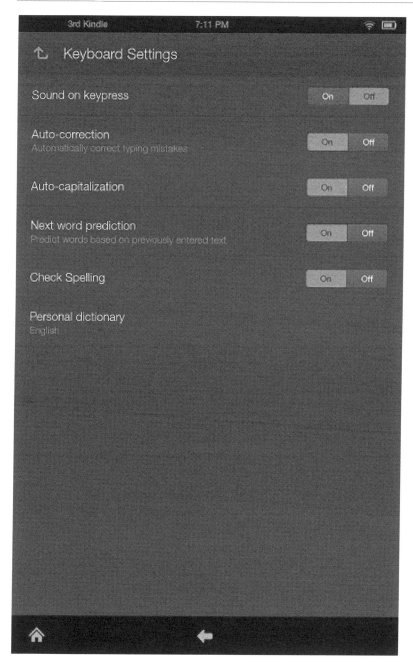

Figure 26: Keyboard Settings Screen

16. Setting Up a Lockscreen Password

You may wish to set up a lockscreen password to prevent unauthorized access to your device. The device will ask you for your password every time that you try to unlock it. To set up a lockscreen password:

1. Touch the time at the top of the screen and slide your finger down. The Quick Settings Banner appears.

2. Touch the ⚙ icon. The Settings screen appears.

3. Touch **Security**. The Security Settings screen appears, as shown in **Figure 27**.

4. Touch the [On | Off] switch next to 'Lock Screen Password'. The Lock Screen Password screen appears, as shown in **Figure 28**.

5. Enter a PIN, which must be at least four digits in length. You may also touch the [On | Off] switch next to 'Simple Numeric PIN', if you would like to enter an alphanumeric password.

6. Touch **Finish**. The Lockscreen Password is set up, and will be required to unlock your device.

You may also touch **Require Lock Screen** on the Security Settings screen to set the amount of time that the device should wait after you have locked it before requiring the password. For instance, if you set the Require Lock Screen time to five minutes, and try to unlock it after three minutes, it will not prompt you for your password.

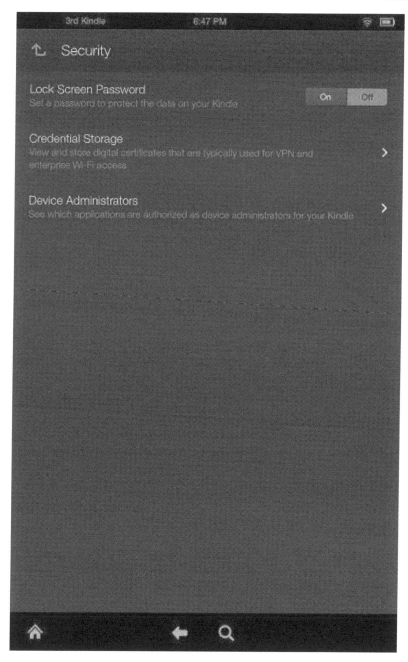

Figure 27: Security Settings Screen

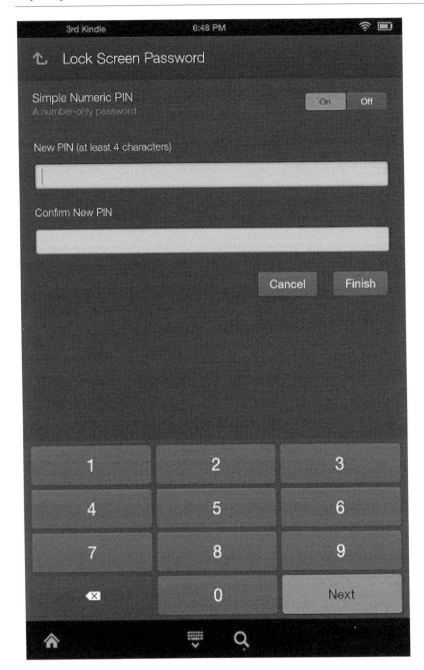

Figure 28: Lock Screen Password Screen

17. Logging In to Your Facebook and Twitter Accounts

The Fire HDX allows you to connect to your Facebook and Twitter accounts, which can be used to share passages while reading, as well as in many other applications. To log in to your Facebook and Twitter accounts:

1. Touch the time at the top of the screen and slide your finger down. The Quick Settings Banner appears.
2. Touch the ⚙ icon. The Settings screen appears.
3. Touch **My Account**. The My Account screen appears, as shown in **Figure 29**.
4. Touch **Social Network Accounts**. The Social Network Accounts screen appears, as shown in **Figure 30**.
5. Touch **Facebook** or **Twitter**. The corresponding credentials screen appears.
6. Enter the credentials associated with your social network account, and touch **Connect**. The social network account is added to your device.

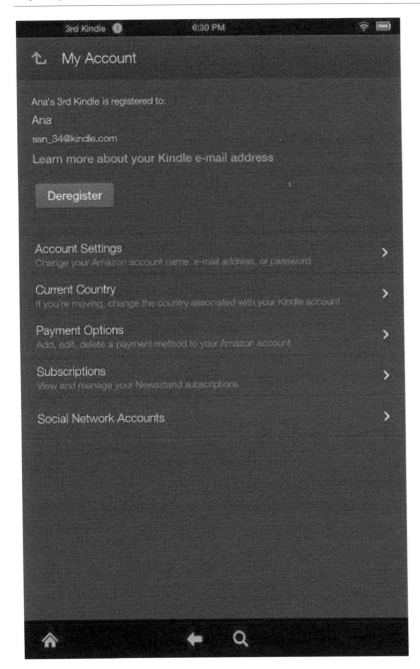

Figure 29: My Account Screen

Figure 30: Social Network Accounts Screen

Tips and Tricks

Table of Contents

1. Maximizing Battery Life

There are several things you can do to increase the battery life of the Kindle Fire HDX:

- Lock the Kindle Fire HDX whenever it is not in use. To lock the device, press the **Power** button on the back of the device once.
- Keep the screen timeout feature set to a small amount of time to dim and turn off the screen when the Kindle Fire HDX is idle. To learn how to change the screen timeout, refer to *"Setting the Screen Timeout"* on page 235.
- Turn down the brightness. To learn how to change brightness settings, refer to *"Adjusting the Brightness"* on page 202.
- Turn off Wi-Fi when it is not in use. To learn how to turn Wi-Fi off, refer to *"Setting Up Wi-Fi"* on page 220.

2. Checking the Amount of Available Memory

To check the amount of available memory at any time:

1. Touch the time at the top of the screen and slide your finger down. The Quick Settings Banner appears.
2. Touch the ![icon] icon. The Settings screen appears.
3. Touch **Device**. The Device settings screen appears.
4. Touch **Storage**. The Storage screen appears, and the amount of available memory is shown, as well as a breakdown of the types of media taking up the space on your device.

3. Freeing Up Memory

There are several actions that can free up memory on the Kindle Fire HDX. Try one or more of the following:

- Archive applications that are no longer needed from the device. Refer to *"Archiving an Application"* on page 191 to learn how.
- Archive any music that you do not currently need. Refer to *"Archiving Music"* on page 109 to learn how.
- Archive any movies or TV shows that you do not currently watch. Refer to *"Archiving Movies and TV Shows"* on page 92 to learn how.
- Remove all temporary internet files. To delete these files:

  1. Touch the time at the top of the screen and slide your finger down. The Quick Settings Banner appears.
  2. Touch the ![icon] icon. The Settings screen appears.
  3. Touch **Applications**. The Application Settings screen appears.
  4. Scroll down and touch **Silk Browser**. The Silk Browser Settings screen appears.
  5. Touch **Clear All Cookie data**, **Clear Cache**, or **Clear History**. The corresponding files are deleted.

4. Searching an eBook for a Word or Phrase Quickly

You can search for a word or phrase in an eBook without typing it. Touch and hold the word in the eBook. The Word menu appears. Touch **More** and then touch **Search in Book**. A list of locations where the word appears is shown. You can also search for a whole phrase by touching and holding a word and dragging your finger to select the rest of the phrase.

5. Viewing the Trailer for a Movie

In order to make a more informed decision when purchasing or renting a movie, you can view its cinematic trailer. To view a movie trailer, touch **Watch Trailer** in the movie description. Refer to *"Browsing Movies and TV Shows in the Video Store"* on page 81 to learn how to browse the Amazon video store.

6. Turning Automatic Music Downloads On or Off

You can set newly purchased music to automatically download to your device, therefore avoiding having to choose every time that you purchase music. To turn automatic music downloads on or off:

1. Touch **Music** at the top of the Library. The Music library appears.
2. Touch the left edge of the screen and slide your finger to the right. The Music Library menu appears.
3. Touch **Settings**. The Music Settings screen appears.
4. Touch the [On Off] switch next to 'Automatic Downloads'. The [On Off] switch appears, and Automatic Downloads are turned on.
5. Touch the [On Off] switch next to 'Automatic Downloads'. The [On Off] switch appears, and Automatic Downloads are turned off.

7. Closing All Tabs at Once in the Silk Browser

In addition to closing one tab at a time, you can also close all tabs simultaneously in the Silk browser. To close all tabs, touch and hold a tab and then touch **Close all tabs**. Once all tabs are closed, the Most Visited screen appears.

8. Deleting a Bookmark in the Silk Browser

Warning: Once a bookmark is deleted, it is gone for good.

Clean up your Bookmarks by deleting unneeded ones. To delete a bookmark from the Bookmarks screen, touch and hold it and then touch **Delete**. A confirmation dialog appears. Touch **OK**. The Bookmark is deleted.

9. Closing Applications Running in the Background

When you return to the Library after using an application, it is left running in the background. Some applications take up a lot of memory and may slow down your Kindle Fire HDX. To close an application running in the background:

Warning: Do not close any running application that has the word 'Kindle' or the *icon next to it. This is a system process and should never be closed.*

1. Touch the time at the top of the screen and slide your finger down. The Quick Settings Banner appears.
2. Touch the icon. The Settings screen appears.
3. Touch **Applications**. The Application Settings screen appears.
4. Touch **Manage All Applications**. A list of running applications appears.
5. Touch an application. The Application Usage data appears.
6. Touch **Force stop**. A confirmation dialog appears.
7. Touch **OK**. The application is closed.

Note: Force-stopping an application will not damage it.

10. Viewing the Back Issues of a Periodical

By default, only the latest issue of a periodical is shown in your Newsstand library. To view all issues of a periodical that you have received on your device, touch and hold the cover of a periodical and touch **Show Back Issues**. All previous issues appear. Touch and hold a cover of any issue and touch **Hide Back Issues**. Only the most recent issue is shown.

11. Connecting the Kindle Fire HDX to a TV

The Fire HDX is able to wirelessly connect to an HD TV by using a feature known as Display Mirroring, which is useful if you would like to watch a movie or TV show on a larger screen. You will need a Miracast adapter in order to connect your device to a TV. Some TV's come with a Miracast adapter built-in. Check with your TV manufacturer to determine if your TV has Miracast capabilities. The adapter may be purchased directly from Amazon. To enable Display Mirroring on your Kindle Fire HDX:

1. Touch the time at the top of the screen and slide your finger down. The Quick Settings Banner appears.
2. Touch the ⚙ icon. The Settings screen appears.
3. Touch **Display & Sounds**. The Display & Sounds screen appears.
4. Touch **Display Mirroring.** The Display Mirroring screen appears and a list of devices available for pairing appears.
5. Touch a TV in the list. The screen on the Kindle Fire HDX is cloned on the selected TV.

12. Displaying the Current Battery Percentage

By default, the Fire HDX only shows an ambiguous battery icon, which does not tell you the exact battery percentage. To display the current battery percentage:

1. Touch the time at the top of the screen and slide your finger down. The Quick Settings Banner appears.
2. Touch the ⚙ icon. The Settings screen appears.
3. Touch **Device**. The Device Setting screen appears.

4. Touch the [On Off] switch next to 'Show Battery Percentage'. The Battery Percentage appears in the upper right-hand corner of the screen. Touch the [On Off] switch next to 'Show Battery Percentage'. The Battery Percentage disappears.

13. Viewing an Article in the Silk Browser in Reading View

The Reading View feature in the Silk Browser allows you to read an article in full-screen mode without any distractions, such as ads, and in a larger, more readable font. To view an article in Reading View, open the news article, and then touch **Reading View**. The article appears in

Reading View. Touch the ⊗ icon in the upper right-hand corner of the screen to exit Reading View at any time.

14. Turning on the Screen Reader for the Visually Impaired

The Screen Reader feature can be used by those who are visually impaired, and will pronounce anything that you touch on the screen. To turn the Screen Reader on:

1. Touch the time at the top of the screen and slide your finger down. The Quick Settings Banner appears.
2. Touch the ⚙ icon. The Settings screen appears.
3. Touch **Accessibility**. The Accessibility Settings screen appears.
4. Touch the [On Off] switch next to 'Screen Reader'. The [On Off] switch appears and the Screen Reader turns on and the Screen Reader tutorial begins to play. You will need to touch every button and item two times quickly to select it while the Screen Reader is turned on.

15. Turning On Closed Captioning

You may turn on Closed Captioning in order to display subtitles on supported videos, which is a feature specifically made for those who are hard of hearing. When browsing the Videos store, each video will indicate whether it is compatible with Closed Captioning. Look under 'Subtitles' in the video description to determine Closed Captioning compatibility. For instance, a video may have **English (cc)** written next to 'Subtitles' to indicate that it is compatible with Closed Captioning. To turn on Closed Captioning:

1. Touch the time at the top of the screen and slide your finger down. The Quick Settings Banner appears.

2. Touch the ⚙ icon. The Settings screen appears.

3. Touch **Accessibility**. The Accessibility Settings screen appears.

4. Touch the [On Off] switch next to 'Closed Captioning'. The [On Off] switch appears and Closed Captioning is turned on.

Troubleshooting

Table of Contents

1. Kindle Fire HDX does not turn on

If the Kindle Fire HDX will not power on, try one of the following:

- **Recharge the battery** - Refer to *"Charging the Kindle Fire HDX"* on page 10 to learn how. Do NOT use the USB port on your computer to charge the Kindle Fire HDX.
- **Replace the battery** - If you purchased the Kindle Fire HDX a long time ago and have charged and discharged the battery approximately 300-400 times, you may need to replace the battery. You will need to contact Amazon to do so. Refer to *"What to do if your problem is not listed here"* on page 258 to learn how.

2. Kindle Fire HDX is not responding

If the Kindle Fire HDX is frozen or is not responding, try one or more of the following. These steps solve most problems on the Kindle Fire HDX:
- **Restart the Kindle Fire HDX** - Press and hold the **Power** button for 20 seconds. The screen goes black, and then **kindle fire** appears. Release the Power button. The Kindle Fire HDX restarts.

- **Remove Media** - Some downloaded applications or music may freeze up the Kindle Fire HDX. Try deleting some of the media after restarting the device. To learn how to delete an application, refer to *"Archiving an Application"* on page 192. You may also reset and erase all data at once by doing the following:

Warning: Any erased data is not recoverable.

1. Touch the time at the top of the screen and slide your finger down. The Quick Settings Banner appears.
2. Touch the ⚙ icon. The Settings screen appears.
3. Touch **Device**. The Device Settings screen appears.
4. Touch **Reset to Factory Defaults**. A confirmation dialog appears.
5. Touch **Reset**. All data is erased and the Kindle Fire HDX is reset to factory defaults.

3. Kindle Fire HDX battery dies too quickly

According to Amazon, the Kindle Fire HDX provides up to 17 hours of only reading or 11 hours of video playback or surfing the web. If you find that the battery is dying considerably faster, turn off Wi-Fi before plugging in the Kindle Fire HDX to charge. Refer to *"Setting Up Wi-Fi"* on page 220 to learn how. Also, turn off Wi-Fi before locking the device and when you are not using it.

4. Cannot access the Web although connected to a Wi-Fi Network

Some Wi-Fi networks, such as those in airports, coffee shops, or hotels, may not require a network password when connecting, but do require authentication once you open the Silk browser. If authentication is required, the 📶 icon appears in the upper right-hand corner of the screen. Touch **Web** and then enter the authentication password to connect to the internet.

5. Screen does not rotate

If the screen does not turn or the full horizontal keyboard is not showing when rotating the Kindle Fire HDX, it may be one of these issues:

- The application does not support the horizontal view.
- The Kindle Fire HDX is lying flat while being rotated. Hold the Kindle Fire HDX upright for the view to change in applications that support it.

- Screen rotation is locked. Touch the time at the top of the screen and slide your finger down. Then, touch the 🔒 icon. The 🔄 icon appears and screen rotation is unlocked.

6. Touchscreen does not respond as expected

If the touchscreen does not perform the desired functions or does not work at all, try the following:

- Remove the screen protector, if you use one.
- Make sure your hands are clean and dry. Oily fingers can make the screen dirty and unresponsive.
- Restart the Kindle Fire HDX.
- Make sure that the touchscreen does not come in contact with anything but skin. Scratches on the screen are permanent and may cause malfunction.

7. Computer does not recognize the Kindle Fire HDX

If your computer does not recognize the device when you connect it, it may be one of these issues:

- You are using an incompatible cable. Use only the USB cable that came with your Kindle Fire HDX to connect the device to your computer.
- You are using a USB hub. Connect the device directly to the computer, since some USB hubs will not be able to recognize the Fire HDX.
- You are using Windows XP or earlier. You need to install Windows Media Player 11 or later in order for your computer to recognize the Kindle Fire HDX.

8. Photo or video does not display

If the Kindle Fire HDX cannot open a photo or video, the file type is most likely not supported. Supported file types include:

Images

- BMP
- GIF
- JPEG
- PNG

Videos

- 3GP
- MP4
- VP8

9. Cannot view the time on the lock screen

The time is not displayed on the Lock screen because the Kindle Fire HDX comes with ads. You may remove the ads for a fee of $15 in order to view the time without unlocking the device. This section does not apply to you if you purchased a Kindle Fire HDX without special offers.

10. Media in the Cloud is not available for streaming

If you first registered the Fire HDX to a specific user, and then de-registered it, and registered it to that user again, you will not be able to stream content that is not already on the device for 180 days. Try to register it to the user account that you will be using as your main account when you first receive the device.

11. What to do if your problem is not listed here

If you could not resolve your issue, contact customer service using one of the following methods:

- If you are in the U.S., call **1-866-321-8851**.
- If you are outside the U.S., call **1-206-266-0927**.
- Email Kindle at **kindle-cs-support@amazon.com**
- Visit **http://www.amazon.com/kindlesupport**.
- Use the Mayday feature by touching the time at the top of the screen, sliding your finger down, and then touching **Mayday**. An Amazon representative will assist you.

Index

Other Books from the Author of the Help Me Series, Charles Hughes

Help Me! Guide to the iPhone 5S

Help Me! Guide to the Nexus 7

Help Me! Guide to the Galaxy S4

Help Me! Guide to the Kindle Fire HD

Help Me! Guide to the HTC One

Help Me! Guide to the iPhone 4

Help Me! Guide to the iPod Touch

Help Me! Guide to the iPad Mini

Help Me! Guide to the Kindle Touch

Help Me! Guide to the Samsumg Galaxy Note

Help Me! Guide to the iPad Air

Help Me! Guide to the Kindle Fire HDX

Author: Charles Hughes

This book is also available in electronic format from Amazon.com

Made in the USA
Lexington, KY
30 December 2013